PASSION *and* ICE

PASSION *and* ICE

LEADING THROUGH VALUES

Stephen F. Stefano

CHAPEL HILL
PRESS, INC.

ISBN: 978-1-59715-050-7
Library of Congress Catalog Number: 2008922014

First Printing

Dedication

Passion and ICE: Leading through Values is dedicated to the three
most important women I know and love. The first is my mother,
Dolores, who carried me physically for the first nine months of
my life and then carried me emotionally from my childhood into
my adult years. The second is my wife, Denise, who I have known
since I was fifteen years old and who has carried and supported me
ever since. Last but not least is my daughter, Jackie, "the apple of
my eye," who I know will carry the values of passion and ICE into
her life and into the lives of many others.

Cary, North Carolina
August 2007

Contents

Foreword

On Wednesday, July 25, 2007, I called my buddy "Little Stevie" as I always do to wish him a great day on his birthday! I should note that he never forgets my special day either. But Steve has an advantage—my birthday and his wife, Denise's, birthday are on the same day. So if he forgets *that* date, he is up the creek without a paddle!

Following my birthday greeting this year, Steve relayed the exciting news that he had just completed writing a book on leadership. I replied, "It's about time!" I have heard Steve speak within the pharmaceutical industry over a dozen times—motivating pharma reps and execs with a strong dose of passion while sharing his valuable experiences using humorous anecdotes and in-your-face challenges. Without fail, his audience absorbs his every syllable. Why? Because anyone who knows Steve knows that he walks the talk—and he talks candidly about where he has walked.

Stevie and I grew up together in the same town just outside Philadelphia—Lansdowne, Pennsylvania. And we had the same strict Italian upbringing. So you might say we were cut from the same cloth. Whether it was in the water or from the streets, our lives were molded from the same set of values and priorities: belief in God; love of family; passion for people; and a work ethic to succeed, do the right thing, take a leadership role, and give back to the community.

I have known Stevie for the better part of four decades. We first met when we were eight years old playing baseball. I always wanted to be on his team regardless of the sport because even at that young age, Stevie had a unique way of leading his team to victory—and not just with his bat or jump shot.

Our paths crossed only during those fun summer months because we attended different grade schools, high schools, and colleges, and eventually he and I moved on into different walks of life. Steve climbed the corporate ladder, relocating to North Carolina, and built a very successful career in the pharmaceutical world.

I, on the other hand, remained in the Philadelphia area and pursued my goal of building a sports medicine empire. After I sold that business, I chased another dream of winning the NBA world championship title with the Philadelphia 76ers. Oh, how close we came in 2001!

During my tenure as president of the Philadelphia team, our paths crossed again—and never stop crossing! Steve had hired me to speak to a select group of his customers at the prestigious Franklin Institute in Philadelphia. Since that engagement, I've joined Steve for numerous GlaxoSmithKline gatherings to fire up his troops and entertain his customers.

But ironically, I always received as much motivational mojo as I dished out. The motivation didn't come from the standing ovations or the convivial meet-and-greets, great booster shots for anyone's sense of self-worth, but from listening to the inspiring stories of the animated guy standing on stage before me, then watching Steve interact with his staff throughout the meetings after the spotlight was turned off.

In *Passion and ICE: Leading through Values*, Steve also speaks about pride and passion and a sense of purpose. He uses entertaining stories and engaging thoughts to motivate his readers to take action. And he believes his formula for leadership success is applicable to all walks of life. But, as he so succinctly notes, it is vital that you take that first step in the walk—not just talk about it. It is the start that stops most people. Well, I know firsthand that at GSK Steve practices what he preaches, and now he's taking the huge step of sharing his thoughts with the world in *Passion and ICE*.

And I repeat, "It's about time!"

Steve and I are all about creating a sense of urgency in pursuing passions. In fact, in my Ten Commandments of Customer Service, my Tenth Commandment is: "Do It Now!" (Pat Croce, with Bill Lyons, *I Feel Great and You Will Too!* [2000]; New York: Fireside Edition, Simon & Schuster, 2001). In one of my books I even noted Steve's success with GlaxoSmithKline's Orange Card as a sterling example of that.

Steve and his team were charged with the goal of developing a practical solution to the complex issue of providing access to medicines for needy senior citizens. The fact is, according to Steve, that there were millions of Medicare patients (sixty-five years and older) who did not have prescription drug coverage. It's amazing and sadly ironic that there was such negligible drug coverage for the people who need medicines the most.

So in the summer of 2001, within just three months of accepting this exciting challenge, Steve and his team launched their revolutionary answer: the GSK Orange Card, orange being GSK's corporate color. The Orange Card provided access to discounts for all of GSK's products at pharmacy counters across the country to all of those needy grandparents and other seniors.

The GSK Orange Card was a resounding success for the company. It was loved by the press, applauded by politicians, and embraced by senior citizens themselves. Eventually it was copied by many of GSK's competitors—and imitation is a sure sign of approval.

Is it any wonder, then, why I could not wait for Steve to pen his words on paper? Most people say, "You can't do this" or "That won't work." Steve asks, "How can we do it?" or "What will make it work?" He is a living, breathing example that dreams and desires do come true. It is his "Never-say-never" attitude with a punch of positive enthusiasm, a pinch of passion, and a spoonful of compassion that make Steve's approach to life—and leadership—so irresistible. I wanted to read all about it!

One final note: If you are a parent like me, you will be tickled twice when you read "Daddy's Little Girl," the last chapter of *Passion and ICE*. But please don't do what I did in high school and read the last chapter first. Begin now at chapter 1, "Oatmeal," to take the first step to strengthen the leadership-muscles in you. Little Stevie has opened a door.

Carpe diem! "It's about time!"

Do It Now.

Pat Croce
August 2007

Preface

This book is not about the pharmaceutical industry, and it is not about GlaxoSmithKline per se. Nor is it a book whose purpose is to promote the value of our company or the benefits of our medicines. Make no mistake about it: I believe deeply in the mission of our organization, and I am most thankful that my company has afforded me the many opportunities and special mentors I describe in *Passion and ICE*.

This book, however, is simply about values in leadership. Those values transcend my career at GlaxoSmithKline and extend back to experiences from my childhood, some of which I describe here as having had a significant impact on my leadership beliefs today. I tell several stories from my memory bank because I believe that stories provide illustrative and memorable imprints for the reader to use. Reading my stories is extremely practical for you in your daily life at work, at home, and in the community.

My values in leadership center on a simple, hearty recipe whose ingredients are integrity, courage, and empathy wrapped in a crust of passion. It is truly the staff of life because it provides you, the reader with a simple, nourishing meal that will energize you around leadership values and behaviors. I hope you enjoy taking it in as much as I have enjoyed writing it.

Acknowledgments

Passion and ICE: Leading through Values would not have been possible without the support and encouragement of my friends and family members who took the time to read chapters and excerpts and to offer their thoughts and suggestions. Many of them are mentioned in the stories that develop the idea of *Passion and ICE*.

However, many others, such as Ron and Mary Gionta, Janice Martin, Dick Domann, Alan Metz, Joanne St. John, Robert Veeder, Tricia Schwab, Rusty and Joane Lamberto, David Pernock, Dan Keeney, Mike Gold, and Andy Olcese, took a lot of their time to review this work and to suggest useful insights, and offer energizing encouragement.

I also want to provide special thanks to Ann Lloyd and Donna Brown for their assistance, as well as to Cristina Fernandez for helping me navigate the legal logistics at GlaxoSmithKline.

Finally, I would like to thank my editor, Linda W. Hobson, and my publisher, Chapel Hill Press, for the objectivity and professionalism that helped me turn a dream into a reality.

Man is immortal, not because

he alone among creatures

has an inexhaustible voice,

but because he has

a soul,

a spirit capable of compassion and

sacrifice and endurance.

WILLIAM FAULKNER
December 10, 1950, upon receiving the Nobel Prize

Chapter One

———

OATMEAL

*W*hy write another book on leadership? So many have already been written in all shapes and sizes—big books, little books, fat books, skinny books—and from so many accomplished authors. Everyone from renowned theorists like Peter Drucker and Stephen Covey to celebrated CEOs such as Lee Iacocca and Jack Welch have marked the business-book turf with ideas about what it takes to be a great leader. So why write another one?

One of the reasons is simple. I wanted to write a book that has a memorable leadership formula—easy to remember and useful to you on those "cold" days when you are under fire. I wanted to create something that sticks to your ribs like oatmeal. I've read many books on how to be a more effective leader. Almost all of them are filled with valuable information, whether researched or anecdotal, but their messages just don't stick. They have no real staying power and let you down as fast as a breakfast of glazed doughnuts and black coffee when you are out there on the field of battle and the rounds are flying by your head.

Forget that their authors spent countless hours researching, validating, and documenting their leadership theories, then compiling them into compelling reads. Their messages don't resonate. These authors hope that middle-level managers and fast-track executives spend twenty to thirty dollars on the book, incorporate their pearls of wisdom into workplace behaviors, then talk up the book, so that they can incorporate millions of dollars in royalties into their bank accounts. I must admit I have often been seduced by seeing the latest *New York Times*–bestselling leadership book with its glitzy cover design lying on an airport newsstand table shortly before I boarded a long flight. Once I read and digest them, however, I find that at the very best I can hardly remember even one or two ideas from each of them.

So my idea was to write a leadership book that has a simple, tried, and tested formula for real leadership. One that is oatmeal-sticky, one that has true staying power. One that is as easy to remember and as easy to incorporate into your daily life as Ben Franklin's truism, "A penny saved is a penny earned," or Harry Truman's promise, "The buck stops here."

The second reason for writing this book is that it comes from someone who actually learned how to lead—through careful observation of my own results, then calibrating for next time; through friendly, helpful feedback; as well as through furious feedback and grievous-hard lessons that sometimes I thought would break me. But I believe in the adage, *Discimus agere agendo*: We learn to do by doing.

This book comes from someone who was given a once-in-a-lifetime chance in a once-in-a-lifetime company, and who seized that opportunity to lead thousands of people. Doing so is a great privilege. I didn't just think about leading or talk about it, I have utilized this simple leadership formula effectively for twenty-plus years in top executive positions at GlaxoSmithKline (GSK), a company that went from nothing to a company that proudly leads the pharmaceutical industry in 2008. As of this writing, Glaxo has a market capitalization of approximately $150 billion. A pharmaceutical giant, it is the eighteenth-largest corporation (by market cap) on the face of the earth.

But twenty years ago, we were a relatively unknown company in the global pharmaceutical industry and almost completely unknown in the United States. Our growth and transformation were unexpected, and I was fortunate to have been able to play a role in our success.

Let me be clear, though. You should know that no one, *no* one, would have predicted that I ever would be in a position to make such an impact and play such a key role—at Glaxo or anywhere else.

When I began my career, almost thirty years ago, no one—not my friends, not my family, not even I—thought that I had the talents, abilities, or brainpower to accomplish what I have accomplished. The truth is that I really don't have that kind of gray matter. You see, I did not then, nor do I possess now the classic

makeup for the corporate world, let alone the makeup to be a successful senior executive for a Fortune 100 company, today one of
the most powerful pharmaceutical companies in the industry.

I don't have a science degree, and I don't have any type of
advanced degree. My sheepskin is a bachelor of arts from St.
Joseph's College, where I majored in political science. When I
was growing up in Philadelphia, I was not surrounded by corporate
people or people who worked in the pharmaceutical industry. Most
of my family and friends worked in blue-collar jobs, primarily in the
newspaper business, or they were self-employed. And when I was
growing up, I was more interested in just getting by than I was in
fulfilling some dream to be a successful business executive. Absolutely no one would have predicted that I would ride this wave of
success at Glaxo to such an interesting and curious shore. And to
get here, I hewed, planed, sanded, and painted my *own* surfboard.
That's part of my story in this company that provides important
medicines to people from nations on each of the seven seas.

Today, my 1980 résumé would have offered me no chance of
employment with GlaxoSmithKline. Today I would not have
made it through the screening process for an entry-level sales
position. My résumé today would be good raw material for a paper
airplane aimed at the circular file.

But back then I did get a sales position at Glaxo, and I am
really proud that I did and proud of what my company has accomplished. Most important, I am proud of how I learned to be a top
leader, and that's what I want to share with you. Because you can
do it, too!

Third, and arguably the most important reason to write this book, is to thank the people who have helped me along the way. The individuals in this book are my true mentors, people who have shared their valuable time and leadership insights with me. They have done this either directly and explicitly through their words or indirectly and implicitly through their actions. In both cases their lessons have been powerful. The wisdom and living examples these people have shared with me along this journey have enabled me to realize success in leading men and women to do their very best.

But I must give myself a little bit of the credit, too. While I am well aware of the impact that the valuable teachings of my mentors have had on me, I am also cognizant of my own abilities for self-study, introspection, and continual improvement. That comes, perhaps, from many years of playing competitive sports. Whatever the source, these three abilities have allowed me to listen to and accept constructive criticism.

How easy it is for us to block out the tough news, to become defensive when someone points out an area for improvement, or to wallow in the comfort of denial when a colleague identifies a critical flaw in our decision making or action. The most comfortable near-term approach is to turn a deaf ear, whereas the least comfortable reaction but best thing to do is to listen to the constructive advice of those you trust. The greatest means to improvement is not only to listen to the honest advice of others, but also to be thoughtful, open-minded, and receptive to that advice.

For example, in 1996 a young collegiate golfer from Stanford

University, after winning three consecutive U.S. amateur championships, left his school to join the PGA Tour. He was billed as a "can't-miss" prospect; unlike many of his predecessors, he lived up to his reputation. His name? Eldrick Woods.

Tiger burst onto the Tour in late September 1996, and within two months he won his first PGA event, the Las Vegas International. In 1997, he won his first major, the Masters, by 12 strokes. Before the end of 1998, Tiger had won 6 of the first 21 PGA tournaments he entered, and was the number-one-ranked player in the world. In addition, he signed multimillion-dollar, multi-year contracts with Nike, Titleist, American Express, and Rolex, to name a few.

Known as an exceptionally long hitter with a fiercely competitive spirit and a surgeon's touch around the greens, Tiger knew, however, that his lack of precision off the tee as well as distance inconsistency with his short irons would make it very difficult for him to realize his ultimate goal of winning all four major championships: the Masters, the U.S. Open, the British Open, and the PGA Championship; he wanted to be recognized as the greatest golfer of all time.

So Tiger practiced introspection. He came to understand his strengths and weaknesses and had the courage to change. Every time he was interviewed and questioned about his strategy to improve his swing, Tiger responded by telling the reporter that he could not meet his goals unless he brought more consistency to his game. As a result, the year 2000 saw Tiger complete the career grand slam—the youngest person ever to do it. He won three championships, the U.S. Open and the British Open by the largest margins ever and the PGA in a monumental sudden-death playoff. By the way, in case you are counting, he won seven other tournaments in 2000. If the number-one player on the PGA Tour can admit and address his personal weaknesses, we can follow that example in working toward our own goals.

As it relates to improving our skills and effectiveness, I have an analogy I love to use with the people who work with me. First, I ask them whether they listen to the people they trust.

"Oh, yes," they answer agreeably.

"Good," I follow up. "Then I guess you'll always be able to avoid that nasty disease that affects businesspeople, 'Hippopotamus disease.'"

Typically they look at me with an expression of bewilderment and may be thinking, "What the hell is Hippopotamus disease?"

"Ah, yes," I conclude. "It's a serious, transforming ailment in which your ability to listen has become impaired because, just like the hippopotamus, you now have two little ears and one big mouth."

Earlier I said that one reason I wrote this book is that I am someone who has "done it." I have used the simple ICE Model I'll explain in subsequent chapters to attain success and make helpful contributions at Glaxo, so this is not a bunch of empty theory about leadership. My leadership model works.

Remember, this model comes from someone who never had any formal training to lead anybody, let alone thousands of people. My promotions, my successions at Glaxo, were a function of "battlefield opportunities." These promotions occur when you are placed in a business situation that is experiencing explosive growth and the organization is truly desperate to find people who will step up and accept new challenges. So individuals simply get assigned to lead. Just as on the field of battle, the circumstances require someone to accept more responsibility and lead the troops out of a leadership vacuum.

That is exactly what happened to me. I was the beneficiary of the privilege to lead for two reasons: the explosive growth of our company and the dynamic changes in how our industry markets medicines. That fast organic growth and those external changes impinging upon the industry enabled me to grow from individual contributor to corporate officer.

As a sales representative, I witnessed both good and bad leadership from managers above and around me, so I experienced, firsthand, both positive and negative behaviors. As a corporate officer, someone who is responsible for the financial performance of our company and for the livelihoods of thousands of employees, I have also seen close to all of it when it comes to leadership styles, leadership values, and leadership effectiveness—from the very good to the very bad. Today, I serve as an officer and member of the company's U.S. Pharmaceutical Operating Committee for a multibillion-dollar corporation.

But twenty-five years ago, Glaxo, as it was known then, was a mere $6 million company in the United States, and I was just a lonely sales representative in the Philadelphia area.

Today, we develop and market novel, important medicines such as Advair for asthma, Tykerb for breast cancer, Coreg for congestive heart failure, and Lamictal to prevent epileptic seizures. Currently, these are just four of our stable of blockbuster medicines that sell in excess of $1 billion annually in the United States. And as of this writing, we may be on the verge of launching four significant new medicines for the treatment of cancer.

In contrast to the wonderful medicines we sell today and the important breakthroughs we will introduce tomorrow, twenty-five-plus years ago when I began my career as a sales representative, I was selling two "medicines"—one of them a vitamin, Vicon-C, and, believe it or not, the other a rectal cream, Corticaine Cream!

So it has been quite a journey from $6 million to $20 billion, from contributor to leader, and from detailing a product for hemorrhoids to marketing medicines for cancer. Throughout this journey GSK has provided wonderful fellowship for me. Let me share with you how it all got started. It's a terrific story. I was not really looking for a job when this opportunity came my way. No question, it was pure luck.

Glaxo had just decided to expand into the U.S. market, and they wanted to hire sales representatives. Since they were virtually unknown in the United States, however, they were not really able to attract experienced talent from the sales forces of the other major U.S. pharmaceutical companies. They opted instead to dip into a different talent pool, targeting young, energetic people with backgrounds in health care or people with sales experience and selling talent.

One of my closest friends at the time, Tony Capello, had just completed pharmacy school at the Philadelphia College of Pharmacy and Sciences, the oldest and one of the most prestigious pharmacy schools in the United States. He was working in our neighborhood pharmacy when the Glaxo district sales manager was making recruiting rounds and stopped off at his store to ask him whether he or anyone he knew might have an interest in pharmaceutical sales. Tony had no interest in sales, but he told this man that he knew someone who might be a good fit for this kind of work. He also took one of the district manager's business cards to give to me the next time we were together—usually every weekend. But as it turned out, he completely forgot about the encounter.

Two months later my pharmacist buddy, Tony, along with his wife Therese, my wife Denise, and I were out having dinner at one of our favorite local Italian restaurants when he reached into the inside pocket of his coat to get his wallet, only to come across the forgotten business card. He got a kind of surprised and embarrassed look on his face when he realized what he'd done and told me, "It's not too late to call this guy, Steve. It might be a real good opportunity, you know?" I did, and the process was under way.

After researching the company, having two or three interviews, and going on one ride in the field with a crusty old representative who did everything he could to convince me that I really did not want to be a pharmaceutical sales representative for Glaxo (later he would become one of my biggest supporters), I was completely smitten. I wanted this job, and I wanted it badly. It just felt right. I had a feeling that this job would be a good fit for me.

The interviews went well. My research of the company instilled confidence in me that Glaxo was a solid and respectable organization, and I liked everyone I met. But most important, I believed the job would provide the challenge that was missing from my work up to that time.

Finally, on a Monday evening in late October 1980, I was offered and accepted a job as a pharmaceutical sales representative for Glaxo. I remember it as if it were yesterday. It was one day after my brother's wedding and on the same night that the Philadelphia Phillies defeated the Kansas City Royals in Game Six of the World Series (Steve Carlton pitched a terrific game, and the late Tug McGraw—as only the "Tugger" could do—finished it in dramatic style).

I was just coming off the world's worst hangover from the wedding the night before when I accepted this job. I was very excited and loved having this new opportunity. Intuitively, I knew this would be a terrific chance to have a promising career and to make some good money along the way. A sales job for a pharmaceutical company, complete with salary, bonus, health benefits, and, most important, a brand-new company car, seemed like my pot of gold at the end of the rainbow.

Denise and I had just been married, and all I wanted was a challenging job with a good company, a steady income, and a nice, relaxing, quiet life. This was it, you see? I was simply a Philly kid through and through, with Philly roots, and just like almost every other Philly kid, my expectations of myself were not that high. This job seemed like the pinnacle of my career aspirations. Maybe someday, after proving myself as a sales representative, I could progress to the next level and become a district manager, like the gentleman who contacted my buddy Tony, but I had no real plans for anything beyond that.

By 1983 Glaxo was blossoming into a successful company in the

United States, thanks mostly to the introduction of our blockbuster medicine Zantac, for duodenal ulcers. We were hiring people like crazy, and now everyone wanted to come and work for us. So in 1984, I got my first big challenge, my big chance to move up in the organization. I was promoted to the home office, in Research Triangle Park, North Carolina, to be associate training manager, a position that catalyzed even more growth for my career.

Two years later, I was asked to start up a new department, Glaxo's Managed Care Department. During this time companies called health maintenance organizations (HMOs) were beginning to have a significant impact on how we marketed our medicines, and negotiating with them on behalf of Glaxo is where I really cut my teeth or "made my bones," as they say in the mob movies.

The success we had in our Managed Care Department, much of which was due to the wonderful, dedicated people who worked with and for me, was another open door for even more responsibility for me at the company. By 1993, I became a general manager for Glaxo, and an officer of the company. From 1993 until today I have maintained those responsibilities while surviving one acquisition, our purchase of Burroughs-Wellcome, as well as our merger with SmithKline.

In addition, from that time forward, I have led the entire sales force, approximately three thousand sales representatives and sales managers, and at one time or another, I have run each of our specialty business units. Leading our specialty business units has entailed full profit-and-loss responsibilities for our oncology, HIV, and neurohealth franchises. Today these are extremely successful business units in our company. And all during these years, I have maintained my responsibilities for the Managed Care Division of GSK. Not bad for a kid from Philly who never had any aspirations or a defined game plan to be a corporate guy.

Now I tell you this not because I need a pat on the back from you or from me. I tell you this because I want you to see that much of my success is founded on on-the-job training I have experienced as I followed this incredibly fortunate career path. The leadership values and practices I have learned have come from facing tough negotiations and decisions, then working through them day after day until one problem was stabilized and I moved onto another. After a while, I recognized that what I was doing formed a definable pattern or model, and that reading about it would be of value to other leaders.

As you read about my simple model called Passion and ICE, I want you to understand and come to believe that this formula is simple, effective, and real—something you can easily adapt to your own needs in leadership positions at any level. For the past twenty-some years that I have been leading individuals or groups of people, I have relied on this formula.

It has enhanced my chances of success, not because of its magic, but because of its authenticity. It comes not simply from the gray matter inside my skull, but from that little pump that beats approximately seventy-two times a minute inside my chest. Passion and ICE are real, because you can't fake passion and you certainly cannot fake Integrity, Courage and Empathy.

Passion, integrity, courage, and empathy are substantial in getting results, and they are as true and as nourishing as oatmeal, a food that sticks to your ribs on a cold winter morning and keeps you going strong until lunchtime. Oatmeal, an old, old food, is especially helpful to us in this new, new century and postmodern age when the stresses posed by meeting our corporate goals can wear down and leave famished the most dedicated managers. That's when a simple, nourishing recipe can revive our brainpower and revive our passion to contribute at our highest levels to a worthy enterprise—like GSK—with integrity, courage, and empathy.

If you're thinking, "Great prose but easier said than done," I hear you, but read on. Then appropriate my simple formula to your work and home life, and make the formula something that sticks to your ribs, too, because I know it works. And through times of trial, it has become better defined and more refined over a quarter-century.

A heart is not judged by
how much you love but by how much
you are loved by others.

THE WIZARD OF OZ

Chapter Two

———

SEVENTY-TWO BEATS

*I*n the business world, how does someone find their passion? How does someone live with their eyes on the prize, not on the clock? I believe they find their passion by truly understanding and completely internalizing their company's mission.

Living it every minute from the heart. Living it seventy-two beats a minute. Now, that does not simply mean knowing your company's mission statement or the cliché conceived by overpaid consultants that fits nicely under your company's logo.

Instead, passion is about knowing the impact you have on the lives of the constituents or customers you serve. Mission statements are very important. They do give people a sense of how the company views itself, what its function is, and where the company's leadership team believes the organization is going. But mission statements pale in comparison to really understanding the impact that your company makes on people's lives, both externally and internally—the lives of the customers you serve and the lives of the employees who serve your company.

Seeing and hearing the human results of our work are certainly a little easier in our business. We are fortunate because by working in the health-care industry and particularly in pharmaceuticals, we can experience direct and—in many cases—dramatic, positive impacts of our medicines on people's lives. That, however, does not mean that other fields, such as finance, transportation, energy, and communications, do not make significant positive impacts on how people live their lives; it's just that the connection in health care is a little easier and a little clearer to see.

We have only one life to live, and it is precious. When a medicine improves the quality of that life, we want to tell someone about how it happened and how we feel now. So at Glaxo we get a lot of good feedback, and that motivates us to do even better for our customers.

Regardless of the sector or field, the trick as a leader is this: you need to find a way to crystallize the company's mission in your heart, turn the good results your work is getting into human stories, and then communicate them regularly and authentically to the people you lead. You must believe and live your company's value in human terms. And you must communicate the mission and the results, the external and internal feedback, with a passion.

All this requires a conscious decision on your part to interrupt your daily work routines and create opportunities to get up on the bully pulpit and preach the mission with emotion and clarity, with humor and goodwill that will resonate with your people. Second, you gather real-life stories of how your product or service has improved—in some cases, transformed—the lives of your customers, clients, students, patients, or other stakeholders. Tell those stories daily as proof to employees that the company's mission is having an effect, getting results. Together, you are getting somewhere!

If your people see that their leader is articulate and believe that their leader is passionate about the company's mission, they too will be imbued with the same passion and belief. The stories of effective, transforming results of the use of your product or service will ground your employees' own passion and belief in the value of the company's work. Your employees will remember your stories, think about them, and pass them on, thus strengthening their own passion, understanding, and commitment to the mission.

Almost every time I have the privilege to address large groups at GSK, I try to be a preacher of the effects of our company's mission. I do this often. Sometimes at large, prearranged venues like national sales meetings or management meetings, but more often at smaller, more intimate settings that we have consciously created—monthly birthday breakfasts for the employees whose birthdays occur in that particular month, "town halls" or quarterly general assemblies within our division, or when a group of new sales representatives comes to the home office for their initial sales training. Each time I get speaking opportunities like these, I capitalize on them by reminding our people about our mission:

We are in the business of improving people's quality of life or, in many cases, simply giving them more life. As you leave this meeting, take time to reflect on

and consider the importance of that mission. Is there
anything more valuable and honorable than helping
your brother or sister experience a better life—live a
longer life? It's amazing, isn't it, but in our business
we have that ability!

I believe in storytelling. It's been proven to be the most effective method for teachers to teach and for students to learn. After
all, if fables were what Aesop chose to teach by and parables were
what Jesus chose, and if we all remember their stories today, then
stories should still be the sturdy, entertaining bearers of lessons
for us today. Kevin Costner, interviewed on NPR's *Fresh Air* (May
24, 2007), likes Will Shakespeare's stories for their clear ability to
show the way. Costner, who grew up in Compton, California, as
an "average, happy American kid," says that clarity is what motivates him to take a role in a film—the authenticity of the script,
the power of the story. He looks for the vividness of the language
and how well the story is told. Costner likes Shakespeare for
these reasons and because—after the first ten minutes it takes the
actor's ear to break through the old style of the language—the
playwright understands human nature so well that that translates
lucidly to the dilemmas we face today.

In Kevin Costner's 2007 role as Mr. Brooks, he sees his job just
this way—portraying a man facing a dilemma, a man wanting two
antithetical things, thus being tempted and torn in two opposite
directions at once. Here again, unlike the theories of industrial
psychology or management, stories communicate best, most
directly, our struggles, dilemmas, temptations, reasons, decisions,

second-guessing, and results—positive and negative. Thus, they point the way most economically and effectively.

So I tell our people stories of customers we have helped and employees who have been assisted and encouraged to do their personal best at GSK. I describe in detail what that help has meant to them. I use humor and description so that they will have a colorful hook by which to hang the story on their memory-board.

Then I tell a very personal story.

My story shows why I have such a burning passion today about our business. The events of this story dramatically changed how I look at our company, how I view our industry, and how I communicate what it is that we do.

In 1994 I was a very young, very green, thirty-nine-year-old senior executive for Glaxo. The truth is that I was in way over my head, but, as I said before, sometimes battlefield promotions place you in a leadership role well beyond your training. A year earlier, I had been promoted to the position of general manager of our Health Management Division. This division of about six hundred people was responsible for negotiating coverage and access for Glaxo's products in what we now call Managed Markets, organizations that either purchase or reimburse for large amounts of Glaxo's medicines. Our customers included hospitals, health maintenance organizations (HMOs), insurance companies, pharmaceutical wholesalers, and even state governments and the federal government. Any of these organizations could affect and effect access of our medicines to the ultimate user—the patient.

As a relatively young person who was experiencing wonderful, yet very opportunistic advancement in this high-growth company,

I believed that my passion for Glaxo's mission was fueled by my fiercely competitive nature, my desire to succeed, my sense of self-importance, and my thirst to contribute. And to some degree all of those did contribute to my passion. All of these things were important to me, and they did fuel my passion for the company where I worked and the job that I did. But the fuel was also a poison cocktail of blind ambition, projection, and megalomania—drunk down easily by youth!

It was a beautiful, fall Sunday in North Carolina, with clear, light-blue skies and plenty of fresh air to breathe under a canopy of trees turning yellow, orange, and crimson. The harvest was in, but the lawns, hedges, pines, and golf courses were richly green. You have to live in North Carolina to experience an autumn day like this one. The heady smell of sunlight on pine needles is way too vivid and beautiful to simply describe and give you the full effect.

I had just returned from a terrific vacation golf trip with my good friend Bobby Clampett, the ex-PGA professional who now announces golf for one of the major television stations, and another close friend, John Strasser, a veterinarian who now takes care of our two dogs, Molly, a Siberian husky, and Frankie, an Akita. We had taken Bobby's private plane to Deerfield, a golf course in Tennessee that he had just completed designing. Life was great—not a care in the world. Here I was, an executive with a world-class pharmaceutical company, and I was flying to golf courses on a private plane with a professional golfer!

I hadn't been home an hour before I got a call from my brother, John, who is three years older than I. Although John and I are similar in many ways, including our physical appearance, we couldn't be more different in gray matter and personality. John is a very successful neonatologist, an intellectual, quiet and reflective. I, on the other hand....

John sounded very concerned, wasting no time with small talk. He told me, "Steve, you need to get home right now and talk to Dad because apparently he's having some serious health problems. He looks absolutely terrible, and being the stubborn guy that he is, he's refusing everyone's, including Mom's, advice to see a doctor and get some help. You're the only one Dad'll listen to, Steve, and you're our only chance of convincing him to get some help."

I knew John was right, because in addition to my father being my dad, he was also my best friend in life. We had a certain bond and connection, a close relationship that enabled us to relate in a special way. I knew it was unusual among fathers and sons to be so close. I think it came from our having similar personalities and thus knowing intuitively how the other one thought and processed information.

As a result, I knew Dad was not just being stubborn. I knew that deep down he was scared—very, very scared. He was aware something was wrong, but he was in complete denial. Just as I would be, Dad was frightened to find out how sick he really was.

My dad was always like that. He avoided going to doctors, even for a simple annual check-up, because he did not want to face the possibility of bad news about his health. Although he was a strong person in many ways, including his beliefs and his devotion to his family, when it came to facing the truth about his own health, he was weak, very weak.

On the Monday after my brother's phone call, I boarded a

plane to Philadelphia to follow John's advice and confront my father. When I walked into my parents' house and saw my father, I was stunned. I felt like I'd been hit with a heavyweight fighter's left hook. My knees actually buckled, and I had to sit down fast.

My dad always had a big, proud, handsome, tanned, and powerful presence, but now he was a mere shadow of himself. He looked thin, gray, unkempt, and unclean. He had a look of defeat on his face. This once proud man appeared now to be a beaten man. I took one look at him and excused myself, escaping to the bathroom so I could collect myself physically and mentally. I needed to formulate a plan to get this scared, stubborn guy to recognize the obvious seriousness of his situation. My goal was simple: get him to see a doctor!

Fortunately, I was successful. After a lot of cajoling, cursing, and pleading, I finally convinced him. It wasn't easy, but I was able to get him to listen and agree. About two weeks later, he and I went to see a physician friend of mine, Dr. Lou Dibacco, who examined my dad from head to toe. It was the first step in what would turn out to be a very interesting journey.

As my brother had suspected, things were very bad; actually, they were even worse than John had thought. By the time my dad agreed to get some help it was too late—way too late.

My dad had paid for this ostrich approach to health care: he was suffering from terminal prostate cancer. In addition to having cancer in his prostate gland, the cancer had metastasized to the bones in his hips, legs, and skull. He was at death's door and knocking very hard.

So what do you do? Do you just sit there, throw in the towel, and watch your father, your best friend, die? We were advised that it was too late for chemotherapy and that it was too late for surgery. The cancer had already spread too far. But my dad's new physician, a urologist, told us there was one option. He said we could try a medicine called Lupron. Lupron is an injectable hormone that works by stopping the body's production of testosterone. If effective, it would slow the tumors' growth and trick the disease into a temporary state of remission. It wasn't a cure, but maybe, just maybe, we could buy him some more time, some more life. No guarantees, just a hope.

Well, it worked! For three years he did pretty well on this treatment. It took a little time and lot of positive reinforcement from my mother, my brother, and me, but little by little, we started to see a positive trend. Dad was making progress. Day by day, he was getting stronger, until after a few weeks he was back to his old self. From death's doorstep in the fall of 1994 until about six months later, the man was back! He was even back to his old bad habits—smoking cigarettes, drinking Budweisers, and hanging out with his buddies at the local watering hole. We celebrated three more Thanksgivings and three more Christmases together.

Think about this: he was even able to enjoy three more years of his grandchildren's lives! We watched movies and ballgames and just enjoyed the kinds of simple things we had done together before he became so blighted and enervated by serious illness. For three years, it was unbelievable. Except for visits to his physician for the monthly injection, it was as though he had never been taken ill.

During the summer of 1997, as predicted by my dad's physician, his condition began to deteriorate. The Lupron Dad took to trick the tumors was no longer effective, and now it would only be a matter of months before his cancer would reclaim a hold on him, its final hold. My brother, my mother, and I had known this day was coming, and day by day we could see the toll cancer was taking on my father's physical health as well as on his quality of life.

By late fall, he was unable to walk the ten or fifteen steps from the living room to his usual seat at the head of the dining room table without the aid of a walker. He no longer had much of an appetite, so he began to lose weight and strength rapidly. His face became drawn, and his arms and legs looked like spindles. He spent his remaining days either asleep in his bedroom or lying down, watching television on the living room couch. I could see that it would just be a matter of time, a couple of short months.

My hope was that he would make it through Christmas. I just wanted to spend one more holiday season with my hero, my best friend.

As Christmas 1997 approached, I became anxious. Denise, Jackie, and I had made our plans to drive from North Carolina to my parents'. We would leave about five or six days before Christmas and stay through the New Year. We all knew Dad would not be around much longer, so we wanted to spend as much time as we could with him during his last holiday season.

On a Sunday night about two weeks before we were scheduled to drive to Philly, Denise woke me up complaining of severe stomach pains. I told her she probably had some kind of intestinal virus or that she had eaten something that disagreed with her and she should try to go back to sleep. About an hour later, though, she woke me up again and demanded that I take her to the emergency room. "Steve, this is the worst pain I have ever experienced—a lot worse than labor pains!" At the emergency room of WakeMed, Denise was writhing in so much pain that painkillers were not even making a dent in her discomfort.

The emergency room physicians concluded that she probably had a ruptured appendix, so they prepped her and took her to surgery. The surgeon on call gave me all the consensual paperwork to read and sign and then told me that this was a quick and routine procedure. Four hours later I was still sitting in the waiting room, now joined by Chris Carney, his wife Cindy, and Kim Crutchfield, all special friends who had found out that Denise was in the hospital, but I still had no news about my wife. Finally the surgeon came out and told me, "Denise's situation and the surgery are much more complicated than what I originally expected.

"She didn't have appendicitis. Instead her extreme pain is the result of an enstrangulation of her large intestine. The wall of her stomach ruptured a while back, and a piece of her intestine slipped through the opening. Over a short period of time the stomach wall closed around it. Left untreated, the intestine would have ruptured, causing leakage of bacteria into her stomach cavity, the peritoneum. The result would have been peritonitis, a life-threatening infection. It's pretty serious, but we're taking care of it—won't be much longer and you can see her. She's a strong person!"

What started out as an apparent stomachache resulted in a serious one-week hospital stay and a relatively long recovery. When Denise was discharged from the hospital, the surgeon recommended that rest and very limited physical activities were best for her recovery. He also advised that we should not plan any prolonged or stressful travel. I told him that we needed to get to Philadelphia because of my dad's dire situation.

Although he understood the gravity of my dad's condition and my deep desire to get there, he advised strongly against the eight-hour car ride that Denise would have to endure. I asked him about flying, and again he advised against it because he was concerned that airport crowds, especially during the holiday season, could result in jostling or bumping that might affect her incision. Wow, now I was really stuck! I had no idea what I was going to do.

Soon a solution and answer to my prayers surfaced, and it came to me from the hands and heart of Glaxo's president, Bob Ingram.

Bob had come to us from Merck in the early 1990s. He was personally recruited by our chief executive at the time, Dr. Ernie Mario, who, in my opinion, is easily the best CEO this industry has seen in thirty years. Ingram was a star at Merck, and most people there believed he would be a lifer. Under the mentorship of Dr. Roy Vagelos, Merck's chief executive, Bob was one of two or three people in line for the top spot at what was then listed by *Fortune* magazine as America's Most-Admired Company. It was through Dr. Mario's charisma and persuasion that we were able to get Bob to leave Merck and join Glaxo.

Ernie's commitment to bringing Ingram into our organization was just what the doctor ordered—no pun intended. Although Glaxo was an extremely successful company, we needed someone who would provide us with leadership and organizational stewardship as we transitioned from a young commercial organization to one that could deliver consistent and predictable results year after year. We were riding on the coattails of our blockbuster Zantac, but we needed to build an organization that would be successful as we transitioned from a one-product wonder to a fully integrated research, development, and commercial machine—in other words, moving into post-Zantac days.

Ingram was exactly the type of executive our company needed to make such a transition. It was almost as if he were right out of central casting for the role. Picture a guy in his early fifties with the right mixture of gray hair and a receding hairline. We used to joke that he had "great corporate hair." He was always impeccably dressed and could speak eloquently about even the most challenging issues facing our industry. When he was at Merck, Bob served for many years as vice president of their Federal Affairs department, a department designed to influence health-care policy and legislation on Capitol Hill.

Prior to Merck's establishment of this function, it was unusual for a pharmaceutical company to employ a group whose role would be to influence federal legislation that could affect their business. Up until this time, we left all of that work to our trade organization, The Pharmaceutical Manufacturers of America, also known as PMA. Under Ingram's leadership, Merck's efforts made dramatic differences in how the bills were written and what they said, and Ingram established himself as an effective lobbyist and pharmaceutical executive. He built many long-standing relationships so that even today he is on a first-name basis with our surviving U.S. presidents, with many influential senators and congresspersons, as well as with celebrated CEOs of *Fortune* 100 companies. Bob Ingram is a "Hall-of-Famer" in the pharmaceutical industry.

Once Ingram found out about my dilemma, it took him about a second to call me and offer the solution that would enable us to get back to Philly. He told me that he would have a corporate jet, a Gulfstream IV that was usually only commissioned for our most senior people, like Dr. Mario and Bob, available for Denise, Jackie, and me to get home. The only caveat, according to Bob, was that Denise's surgeon had to approve. Her surgeon said it was fine, and a couple of days later we were on our way.

It is no wonder that I have such a passion for our business, and for leaders like Bob who somehow find avenues to help people. There is no bonus check, stock option grant, or salary increase that could ever compare with that unforgettable gift that he provided to us. With that one thoughtful gift, that one thoughtful gesture, he enabled us to spend one more Christmas with my father.

This story about my Dad's battle with terminal cancer is a terrific reinforcement of what it is that we do—our mission to improve people's quality of life or, as in this case, simply give them more life.

A medicine, Lupron, enabled all of this to happen. When I think about that, it truly helps me realize our own mission at GSK, and it rekindles a passion in me for this work we do.

I often think, *What would I give for three more years, no, just three more minutes with my father, my best friend?* And I quickly realize that I would give anything to experience his love and friendship once again. How great is that? How powerful is that? I have a passion today about our business because I experienced firsthand, in a most personal and meaningful way, what caring people in our business and what the right medicine could do for someone whom I loved very much. It bought him time—time for us to spend together.

As you can tell, one of my favorite words is "passion," a feel-good word regardless of the context in which it is used. It brings a good feeling to my heart. I absolutely love being around people with passion.

Today, however, passion is a quality that often gets overlooked. Our new generation of up-and-coming leaders, the thirty-some-things with their MBAs, are prone to think more about what they are accomplishing for themselves instead of what effect their work is having on others. They are so focused on managing the components of their careers and businesses, they forget about the psyche and emotions of the people they lead and the people they serve. They often behave as if passion is part of the valueless soft-stuff in today's fast-paced, data-driven, technology-heavy environment. In a business world where voicemails, emails, and text messaging have all but replaced eyeball-to-eyeball personal contact, passion can dry up and go unencouraged.

Interestingly, data show that passion about one's career is directly related to an individual's chances for financial success. In 1962, a study was conducted of such a direct correlation on 1,500 new college graduates. In this study, the researcher divided the students into two groups. The first group, consisting of 83 percent of the study population, chose their career paths based on the potential to earn significant income. The remainder of the group, 17 percent, chose their career paths based simply on doing what they loved and wanted to do; to them, money was not the issue.

Twenty years later, the researcher revisited the two groups.

The results were impressive, and they validated the impact that passion can have on one's ability to realize financial success. Of the original 1,500 students in the study, the researcher found 101 millionaires; of those 101 millionaires, 100 of them came from the 17 percent group that selected their careers based on what they loved to do.

It's true that passion is not an emotion expressed on cue, yet I believe that all great leaders, regardless of their field—business, military, entertainment, education, law, finance, government, sports, health care, and so forth—must possess, demonstrate, and communicate a passion for their organization's mission, for what they do, and for the people they lead.

There is no question that great leaders must possess the hard skills, the competencies to instill confidence in people; that they must understand the challenges in front of them; and that they must have the talent to survey the environment and analyze the data in order to make good decisions. Obviously, great leaders must know what they are doing, but they must also have a sense of mission propelled by their passion for what they do and for what they know their teams can accomplish.

In many cases their passion for the mission involves an awareness of a higher sense of purpose that transcends the facts and logic of the business case. Great leaders have imagination! Their experience and expertise needs to be fortified by their belief in the mission, which comes back to them through their communicating that mission to the people they lead. They talk with their people, and every time they do so, they talk to themselves as well.

If they do this well, they can energize and drive their teams to a performance level well beyond expectations.

Leaders with passion, those with beliefs in line with the company's mission, those with imagination and a higher sense of purpose are infectious. They are energizing. You get a feeling for their sense of spirit, their positive attitude, and their belief in what they are trying to accomplish. Leaders who are passionate have a magnetism that draws people to them because they possess a positive mental attitude, a belief in the mission that turbo-charges their team's efforts. And leaders with passion, those who are unafraid to express their feelings, those who wear their hearts on their sleeves, are almost always a lot of fun to be around.

In July 2003, GSK launched a new indication for one of its existing prescription medicines, Lamictal. Before this new approval, Lamictal, a relatively small medicine for GSK, was initially approved to be prescribed only for what is called add-on or adjunctive treatment for people with certain types of epilepsy or seizures. Doctors, especially neurologists who were using Lamictal to treat patients with epilepsy, reported that they had started to notice something interesting in some of their patients. They were seeing some reports of a mood-brightening effect in some patients for whom they had prescribed Lamictal. Epileptic patients treated with this medicine were not only getting better physically, they also seemed to be much more upbeat mentally. These anecdotal reports triggered some of our internal medical people in conjunction with external opinion leaders in the field of psychiatry to theorize that Lamictal might have another application, some type of antidepressant quality.

Many times in our business we get a pleasant surprise like this when a medicine unexpectedly proves to be effective for more than just one disease. Once we see a trend from these types of anecdotal reports, we establish a hypothesis and conduct clinical trials under the guidance and direction of the U.S. Food and Drug Administration (FDA). If we can prove our hypothesis is correct and if the FDA agrees with the results of clinical trials, then we can obtain an approval for such new indications.

As luck would have it, in this case the reports from the neurologists were absolutely correct. Lamictal worked well particularly for patients with a very severe and often difficult-to-treat mental illness, bipolar depression. This was an exciting discovery because prior to this new finding, there were few medicines approved in the United States for bipolar depression. We knew that if our studies proved to be successful, and the FDA agreed, then Lamictal would be approved in the United States for treatment of this illness.

This would be a huge commercial success for GSK because it would turn a small medicine for the relatively few people who suffer from epilepsy into a potential blockbuster for the many who have bipolar depressive illness. More important, we at GSK were excited about the prospect of this opportunity because in our country there are approximately 3 million people who suffer from bipolar depression, and the disease does not discriminate. It strikes the young adult as well as the elderly. Its prevalence is similar in males and females as well as in Caucasians and people of color. It doesn't matter if you are rich or poor; bipolar disease is an equal-opportunity disease.

It is also an extremely mysterious affliction. Not easily understood or diagnosed, its effects can be devastating. Unlike most of us who have our normal ups and downs, bipolar patients suffer from extreme emotional highs, called "mania," and debilitating lows, called "depression." Another name for the disease is manic-depression.

Misdiagnosed or untreated manic depressives can spend day after day in a severely depressed state wherein they are almost unable to function, barely getting out of bed or up off the couch, then can suddenly change, rapidly cycling into a manic state of uninhibited euphoria. In this manic phase, patients will make wild, impulsive decisions like buying exotic sports cars, spending tens of thousands of dollars on jewelry, or rashly investing in businesses in which they have no understanding or expertise. They go on unrestrained shopping sprees, engage in risky sex, or gamble away their savings. Their lives and the lives of the people around them, their co-workers, family, and friends, are drastically impacted as they spiral out of control in this exhausting cycle of uncontrollable highs and debilitating lows.

The most sobering fact about bipolar disease, however, is that a relatively high percentage of these individuals as compared to the general population become so devastated by the uncontrolled nature of their lives that they attempt to commit suicide. Sadly, many of them succeed.

Right before July 2003, the FDA had approved Lamictal for its new application. Following FDA approval we convened about five hundred of our sales and marketing people, along with a number of our colleagues from our medical department in Atlanta, to launch our product for its new indication. It was an extremely important meeting, as you can imagine from my description of this serious disease and how clearly we had seen the benefits of our medicine in fighting it in the clinical trials.

Pharmaceutical companies typically will convene their sales, marketing, and medical people at such launches to educate and motivate their teams about newly approved medicines or newly approved uses for their existing medicines. Usually the venue is a nice hotel in a resort area or a major city so that our sales representatives are comfortable and nothing stands in the way of their learning about the medicine and its indication or their enthusiasm for the new product. There is a method to our madness!

In this case, though, we could not have picked a worse hotel or, for that matter, a worse location for this very important meeting. Remember, it was July and we had picked Atlanta. Need I say more? In addition to selecting one of the hottest and most humid cities on the East Coast, unfortunately there were some problems at this hotel.

So here we were on the first night, typically a pleasant, relaxing, and motivating reception night, and my Neurohealth Division was anything but pleasant and relaxed. Instead of hundreds of smiles and lots of high-fives, I was the target of their valid complaints: "The rooms are dirty, Steve!" "The air conditioning is noisy," "The food is cold and blah." On and on it went! They were right, and I was both concerned and embarrassed because here we were ready to launch a very important medicine not only for our company but also for patients who previously had little hope for reducing their illness, but instead of being pumped up, the team had—as my friend Pat Croce would say—the complaint machine firing on all eight cylinders. I hardly slept that night for worrying.

The next day we officially started the launch. Five hundred of our folks were assembled in a large ballroom for the opening general session. In this three-hour segment we presented data on Lamictal for bipolar. We had our scientists describe how they figured out that Lamictal would work for bipolar patients as well as for epileptics. We had our marketing people explain that the information, which they had constructed into compelling sales tools, showed conclusive effectiveness of Lamictal for the maintenance treatment of bipolar depression.

Then we did something completely unexpected and different—a bit of a gamble that could have easily backfired. We had five bipolar patients come up on stage. Each of them was given about fifteen minutes to address our sales representatives and share their personal life stories with them. Each one of these brave individuals discussed the illness passionately and honestly. Each one described graphically how devastating bipolar disease can be. A couple of them even shared stories about themselves and other anonymous bipolar sufferers who had reached the lowest of lows and who had considered ending their nightmare, perhaps through an ingestion of pills, a slash of the wrist, or a death by hanging.

Some of them proudly shared with our group how they had turned their lives around thanks to a medicine and where they were today. One was a published author, and two were holding executive positions with very large and important health-care organizations. Each of them opened up their hearts and revealed their life stories. It was a gamble. We really had no idea what they were going to say. There was no script or editorial control on our part. We wanted them to speak honestly about their families, physicians, friends, and the medicine that helped change their lives and turn their nightmares into dreams.

It was easily the most wonderful and moving experience I have witnessed in my professional career. This real-life experience with patients changed the attitudes of our people and turned what could have been a disastrous meeting into the most successful one I have ever seen in my twenty-five-plus years in this industry. Our sales representatives were totally into it. You could have heard a pin drop in that huge room. They were riveted to their seats, and there was not a dry eye in the house.

When we broke for lunch, you could really sense a complete turnaround in the team's attitude. Yesterday's complaints about the hotel were now replaced with today's passion and sense of mission about the impact we could have on the lives of patients.

Our employees' new commitment was real, and you could feel it. All it took was a few patients and family members standing before our people and speaking authentically about their desire to improve their lives and the lives of millions of other bipolar patients. All it took was real passion to get a group of mostly Generation X sales representatives to forget their complaints about the hotel and to focus on the impact of Lamictal to further our mission.

As of this writing, Lamictal, just for the treatment of bipolar depression alone, is a major business success for GSK. It is a blockbuster medicine, selling in excess of $2 billion, which is well beyond our industry standard for blockbuster status.

More important, it is a wonderful success for patients and their families. Think about how many are productive and healthy today because our sales representatives with those noisy air conditioning units in a lousy hotel felt the passion of these individuals. It reinforced in me, just like the story of my dad, that when it is real, when it is crystallized in your heart, and when it is communicated to the people you lead, passion has a power and an energy that helps drive ordinary people to extraordinary accomplishments.

When I think about extraordinary accomplishments, I think back to my childhood and to the first real historic event that I remember. I was only six years old. On a bitterly cold January day in 1961 a young, charismatic U.S. president stood confidently before the world and took the oath of office. On that inauguration day, John Kennedy addressed his most important constituency, the citizens of the United States, with a passion that I believe has been unsurpassed by any president since then as he defined for us one of our most important missions.

He told us that before the end of the decade our mission would be to put a man on the moon and return him safely to earth. Now let's put that in perspective. The U.S. space effort at that time was less than stellar. We were way behind the Soviet Union, which had launched a space capsule into orbit around the earth in 1957. Thus, to even imagine that we would not only catch the Soviets, but actually surpass them in eight and a half short years to become the first nation—in July 1969—to put a man on the moon was beyond almost everyone's expectations.

But not Kennedy's. He had a vision, a vivid picture of the completion of the mission, and he conveyed that mission with a passion that was contagious. His goal to get to the moon became a part of every day of our lives during that decade. Kids everywhere talked about becoming astronauts. Each space mission became a newsworthy national event. We followed each and every Gemini and Apollo mission. Space exploration even gave rise to a new genre of television shows. Then, after eight and a half years, we accomplished the mission that at one time had seemed impossible. From a cold winter day in '61 to a warm summer night in '69, we did exactly what President Kennedy had asked us to do. Astronaut Neil Armstrong stepped onto the surface of the moon and returned safely to earth a few days later.

It's amazing how much communal energy can emerge from having a passion about your mission and passionately conveying that mission to the people you lead. That is what leaders do. They identify the mission, they believe in it, and they communicate it with emotion.

Having a passion about what you do is not only vitally important for you as the leader in order for you to keep up your own morale and good health. Your perceived passion is even more critical for the people you lead. When they see your behavior as being totally in line with the words of the company's mission, their perception of that builds confidence in the company, contagious energy for selling your products and/or services, and it is addictive. People sense it. They see it in the passion and commitment in your eyes, they hear it in your voice, and they feel it through your body language.

That is why it is so powerful to express your passion by means of real-life stories every time you get the opportunity to communicate with your team. In my role, I have many opportunities to address our organization, and every time I speak to our group, I leverage those opportunities to passionately share what I believe our mission is. I tell our folks, "In our industry, and especially in our company, it does not matter where you are on the organizational chart. It does not matter whether you are a bench chemist looking through a microscope trying to find a new medicine, or whether you are a sales representative looking through a windshield trying to find a doctor's office. Our mission is clear. We are in the business of improving people's quality of life or—as in my dad's case and in the cases of those millions of people with bipolar disease—simply giving them more life."

Then I pause, survey the room, look several people in the eye, sharing my energy with them, and close by saying, "I ask you to think deeply about the importance of that mission as you leave this room and return to the noble work that makes that mission—that great idea of healing and extending life—a reality for all the men, women, and children we serve."

It's a wise father that knows
his own child.

WILLIAM SHAKESPEARE

Chapter Three

———

FATHER KNOWS BEST

*I*CE. What is ICE? We learned in grade school that ice is the crystallization of water into its solid form. Water consists of two parts hydrogen and one part oxygen. At thirty-two degrees Fahrenheit or zero degrees Centigrade it freezes, becoming ice. My application of "Leadership ICE" is similar—the crystallization of years of learning and experience into three critical leadership elements—Integrity, Courage, and Empathy.

To me, ICE is a simple model that holds the essence of solid leadership values and behavior, something as basic to life as water and as refreshing to the business climate in any corporation as ice cubes in a glass of lemonade on a scorching summer afternoon. The beautiful thing about ICE is that we can practice it in the business environment, social environment, churches and synagogues, or everyday life. Everyone at some point during the day or the week is a leader, and everyone has an opportunity to employ good leadership values and behaviors. Wherever you lead, you are privileged and obligated to do so with high standards and good values, because as a leader you influence the lives of others, and in some cases you influence many lives.

I have encoded the ICE model into my leadership software, and it drives almost all my decision making. In business, it governs all my important decisions and actions, from strategic planning to personnel management. ICE is a blueprint, a recipe for leadership that comes from my working in positions of leadership responsibility, observing how trusted friends and caring mentors lead, and experiencing on-the-job crises for more than twenty-five years. Those experiences have included lots of successes and just as many failures. I prefer to think of failures, however, in a positive way as learning experiences that give me opportunities for growth and improvement—strengthening my ICE muscles.

The most important source of ICE, though, is approximately forty years of heart-to-heart conversations with the best leader I have ever known. He was a true mentor and my best friend in the world. As you may have guessed from reading the previous chapter, he was my dad. From the time I was a little kid right up until he died, he was always there with the right kind of advice. Isn't it funny how people very close to us, the ones we often overlook or take for granted, can have such an impact on how we live our lives?

My dad, John, was born and raised in South Philadelphia. He came into this world on February 6, 1928, the middle son and namesake of John and Angie Stefano. He had two brothers, Jimmy, three years older, and Bobby, nine years younger. He grew up in a blue-collar neighborhood made up mostly of Italian immigrants and first-generation Italian Americans. They believed in the importance of family values, a solid work ethic, pride in their community, and a strong affiliation with their church—not to mention tons of good food and lots of red wine.

My dad was just like everyone else in this closely knit Italian neighborhood where it seemed as if everybody either knew each other or was related to each other. For the most part, the folks in South Philly were pretty conventional. I am told that Dad was neither an excellent student nor a standout athlete. He never became a big man on campus because he never had the opportunity to attend college. In fact, he was fortunate to complete high school. In South Philly at this time, right after the Great Depression, most everyone believed that earning a living or learning a craft was the only way to go. Getting out and getting a job was more important than staying in school. Many of his friends never even came close to finishing high school.

So this very average, very simple guy managed to complete twelve years of school. He graduated from South Catholic High School (today known as Saint John Neuman High School) in 1946. About two years later he married his childhood sweetheart, Dolores, whom he had known since they were five years old since she lived right across the street from him. After serving in the navy for a couple of years during the Korean War, my dad began a career that lasted almost forty years working for the same company, one of Philadelphia's major newspapers, the *Philadelphia Evening Bulletin*. It was the only company he worked for, and he was totally committed to it.

The Bulletin was one of the city's two major newspapers. The other one, the *Philadelphia Inquirer*, unlike *The Bulletin*, is still in existence today. The *Inquirer* has always been a morning paper. As its full name implies, *The Bulletin* was an evening paper. Unfortunately, in 1982 *The Bulletin* went the way of almost every other evening newspaper in major cities. It closed its doors.

Before the advent of cable television, evening newspapers were much more popular than morning papers. If you think back to the fifties and sixties, for those of us who were around back then, there was a good reason for the popularity of evening newspapers. The news was televised only three times a day, around 7:00 a.m., 6:00 p.m., and 11:00 p.m., and there were only three network channels—CBS, NBC, and ABC. So reading the newspaper, particularly an evening edition that included all of the day's news, was important for learning what had happened, and it was also a nice complement to a relaxing cocktail or a cold beer right after work and before dinner.

Unfortunately, that wonderful practice is just a fond memory, and so are evening newspapers. Today, not a single major city in the United States has a viable evening newspaper. People no longer need it. The demand is not there. Today we live in the "Information Age," and there are so many avenues for getting information. You could be at home, at work, in school, on the road, on an airplane, or in a hotel room. All you need to do is turn on cable television, log onto your laptop computer, activate your handheld BlackBerry, or dial your cell phone to get the news as it is happening in real time all day long. So by the time the sun is setting and people have returned to their families and homes, they already know what happened that day throughout the world. The news is not new.

In a way it's a shame. Information technology, though truly a wonderful advance, has resulted in the demise of evening newspapers throughout the country along with the pleasant hour people spent sitting in their living rooms in the late afternoon or early evening quietly sipping a drink and reading their city's evening "rag."

During most of my dad's career, *The Bulletin* was Philly's most circulated newspaper and a major employer in the city. In fact, I can remember, as a kid in the mid-sixties, that the paper's promotional slogan, "Nearly everybody reads *The Bulletin*," was pasted across many highway billboards and proudly displayed across the top of the front page of the paper.

So for almost forty years and right up until the day it closed its doors and went out of business, my father worked for this newspaper, and he loved it. During his tenure, this guy who had no formal education in either journalism or business management rode the wave of *The Bulletin*'s growth and popularity from an entry-level position as an errand boy up to an executive position in which he was responsible for the paper's daily production. He was also responsible for the management of hundreds of employees—the compositors, who cut the lead type used to press the ink onto the paper, and the pressmen, who ran the massive presses that printed and folded the paper.

As with most city newspapers, especially those in the Northeast, all of *The Bulletin*'s craftsmen like the compositors and pressmen were unionized workers. That in and of itself is a difficult
enough management challenge, but it was further complicated by
the fact that my dad also had to manage his two brothers, three
uncles, one cousin, and even his own father, all of whom were
either pressmen or compositors. Like the promotional slogan
"Nearly everybody reads *The Bulletin*," it seemed to me that
"Nearly every Stefano worked at *The Bulletin*."

But what I remember most from this time was the honest
respect that these workers had for my dad, and let me tell you, they
were not an easy bunch to manage. The compositors and to even a
larger extent the pressmen were dyed-in-the-wool union employees. In some ways they were more loyal to each other than to the
company that paid their salaries. They were extremely tough on
their management, and quite frankly they leveraged their solidarity effectively when it came to presenting their demands. During
critical negotiating periods, they were not beyond reproach when
it came to getting what they believed they deserved.

To them any tactic was fair game. For instance, they might
subtly sabotage equipment, creating production slowdowns and
causing thousands of dollars in damage not to mention substantial revenue losses. Or they might conduct a last-minute wildcat
strike, resulting in the newspaper's shutting down production for
days at a time. They had a lot of leverage as well as very little
regard for *The Bulletin*'s management team. To them, many of
the executives who ran the newspaper were an incompetent,
arrogant, elitist group that there was no need to trust or respect.

And they were not shy about showing management just how they felt. Who knows? Maybe they were partly correct.

Yet oddly enough they demonstrated a great deal of respect for my dad. And they appeared to trust him, too, even though he was part of the same management crew for whom they had such disdain, even contempt in some cases. What was different about him that made this group respect him so much?

I believe the reason this relatively simple, average guy exceeded everyone's business expectations and earned unusual trust and respect among the people he managed was that he possessed and demonstrated the qualities of a true leader. He was successful as a leader, not only because he had and exhibited a strong work ethic and a real competence in his business, but also because he understood and modeled core leadership qualities: integrity, courage, and empathy. He knew them, believed them, and lived them. My father truly was the "ICE King," and I was fortunate to learn by his example and latch onto his secret. I did not know it back then, but I know now that his modeling of those values for his people and for me has left a lasting imprint on my approach to leadership.

As a little kid, I watched him in action. Many Sundays we would go to my grandparents' house for a family dinner. Although my grandfather did not drink any alcohol, invariably my dad's brothers, cousin, and uncles, as well as my dad might have a few drinks and engage in discussions and some pretty animated arguments about what was going right and what was wrong at The Bulletin. My dad's older brother, Jim, might have two or even three opinions on the same issue at one time. My dad, however, never lost his composure in these circular debates. Even though he was in the minority defending management's position, he always listened and respected their positions, and he never compromised on decisions that he thought were correct.

Other times, I would accompany my father to the newspaper where I hung out while he did his job. In these settings I witnessed firsthand how he thought and how he operated. By the age of twelve, I realized that he was a man of conviction who, through his actions, earned the respect and trust of the workers whom he managed. They all knew that my dad would be there; he rarely missed a day of work. He also liked to be visible. He took time to walk around and talk to the people he managed. He was approachable on any topic, and he was a terrific listener. He demonstrated honest and caring respect for the people in his departments, but he wasn't soft on people, nor did he capitulate to their positions on issues.

Let's be very clear. As much as these folks were pro-union, my dad was equally pro-management. He had very little time or appreciation for the need of workers to bind together. He believed individuals should speak and act on their own. He believed in people performing to the best of their ability. He thought unions promoted mediocrity in thinking and action, and my dad had absolutely no time for some of their tactics.

So the trust and respect his workers demonstrated for him did not come because he glad-handed around the plant and kowtowed to them on issues. There was something else. They understood that his positions and decisions came from honest and courageous beliefs delivered with empathy and respect for them as men, as individuals. I know this because at his funeral in 1998, sixteen years after *The Bulletin* folded, so many of those same workers were present to show their respect for him, and they were not bashful about telling me, my brother, or my mom how they felt about him.

Clearly my dad had a special leadership gift, though I am not sure he knew it. When he spoke, people listened. When he directed, people followed. When he shared his thoughts and feelings, people engaged and opened up. And most important, when he cared, people believed. Through his leadership makeup of competence and values, he had the ability to influence people to seek and reach a higher level of performance. At the same time, he earned their respect and trust.

Real leaders get people to accomplish things they would not have accomplished without the leader's presence and influence. Look at Vince Lombardi, Mother Teresa, and Winston Churchill—they had this incredible knack of being able to raise the bar of performance and inspire individuals to leap over it, time after time. What is the nature of this knack? They held themselves accountable to a high standard of behavior, and they modeled it in their actions. I have worked directly for a number of leaders like that in my career, people like Jim Butler, Bob Ingram, George Morrow, George Abercrombie, and Chris Viehbacher, all of whom inspired me to a higher level of performance. They are competent, passionate, and they possess and demonstrate key values like integrity, courage, and empathy. Just as I felt with my dad, I knew that I never wanted to disappoint any of them. I'll be telling you about them in more detail later in this book.

I could go on and on with work stories about my dad that demonstrate his practical mastery of leadership, but one story really
stands out for me. Actually, it wasn't something that happened
at *The Bulletin*. It was way more important than that. It had to do
with his primary leadership job, the job of being a father. At the
most important crossroads of my personal and professional life,
August 1984, I was promoted to the position of associate training
manager for Glaxo Inc.

I was preparing to leave my sales position in Philadelphia
and relocate to Research Triangle Park, in North Carolina. I
was excited and, to be honest, I was scared. In this new role,
my primary responsibilities would be to train our newly hired
representatives on a number of Glaxo's medicines. I would also
be interacting with home office personnel, mostly in sales and
marketing. And ultimately I would be managing people.

Previously, I had worked only as an individual contributor—a
salesman. I hoped this promotion was going to be my chance to
demonstrate that I had the competence and skills to grow and
lead within the organization. In the pharmaceutical industry,
sales training positions are very visible jobs that often catalyze
careers quickly into opportunities for higher responsibility. They
are challenging jobs because they require a solid knowledge of the
business, knowledge of our medicines, a keen understanding of
people, and an ability to communicate effectively. They are just
like teachers' jobs, except their salaries are on steroids!

Glaxo had just launched a new product called Zantac, which
was lighting the world on fire, and we were establishing ourselves
as a formidable company in other areas, such as allergy, asthma,

and infectious disease. In addition to Zantac we had also just launched a medicine called Ventolin, for asthma; one called Beconase, for allergic rhinitis; and another one named Zinacef, for certain types of bacterial infections. So in addition to the growth of our revenue line, our sales force was also growing as fast as if not faster than that of any other pharmaceutical company in the United States. My new responsibilities included training all of our new sales representatives on Zantac as well as on our allergy and asthma medicines. Professionally I believed this was going to be an incredible opportunity. I knew this would be my chance to make my mark in the company.

At this same time, I was facing an even more interesting challenge. Denise and I were only weeks away from the birth of our child, Jackie. So here I was, getting ready to start a new job and a new life as a father, yet for the first time ever Denise and I would be living outside the close support and comfort of our friends and family. How could she and I care for our new baby without their help? Although our new home in Raleigh, North Carolina, was only four hundred miles from Philadelphia, to us it seemed like halfway around the world.

My dad's antennae were really high and tuned into my worries. I have a vivid memory of the two of us sitting at the kitchen table engaged in a serious conversation. After a few Budweisers and way too many cigarettes, he reminded me of the importance of making sure that I paid attention to my family. "Steve, they must always be your *first* priority, especially since you and Denise will be in a new and strange environment."

Once he was convinced that I understood that message and

the probable consequences of not following it, he moved onto advice about business. He told me a lot of things, but the one that stayed with me was this: "Someday you may have the opportunity to lead people ... and one day that may be a lot of people. If you get the chance to do that, you should always, *always* remember two things. First, it's a privilege to lead, and second, people don't care how much you know until they know how much you care." (I heard that second phrase from my dad, but learned many years later that it was first uttered by American author, speaker, and leadership expert John C. Maxwell.)

That advice is so simple, so true, and so practical, I have observed over the years. On the face of it, it is good enough and, if followed closely, would produce good leaders. But for me, it was *great* advice because of the context in which my dad had offered it—my boyhood home. Here and at my grandparents' was where I had seen him follow that very advice Sunday after Sunday in the ongoing work discussions veering into and out of arguments with his family members from *The Bulletin*. Not being afraid to engage in discussions with the compositors and pressmen had given my father the opportunity to hone his leadership skills and become the great leader he was.

First, there was his practical, down-to-earth advice about family priorities when my family was in transition—a new child, a new region of the country to live in. There were certainly challenges there!

Then my dad laid out the challenge of leadership by characterizing it as a privilege.

And finally he delivered the punch line about the necessity of caring for the people you lead. I had seen him do that at *The Bulletin* and then tell us over many family dinners at that same kitchen table about difficult experiences at the paper with his compositors and pressmen and how it had all worked out—what they said and what he said; what they wanted and what he would support. The employees, I recalled, had respected and trusted him primarily because they had seen firsthand that my dad cared for them.

The context, the structure, and the delivery of his message to me in August 1984 were no accident then. They reflected the kind of value system he possessed—his integrity, his courage, and his empathy with others. ICE, that is, and now I have made those values into the model I follow for every leadership experience I have: employer/employee, team at home and at work, and extended family. *Father* does *know best in this case*, I thought that night, and it is no wonder that even today, about a decade after he left us and more than twenty-five years since *The Bulletin* closed, I still run into people who say, "Steve, I really loved working for your dad."

There is no on-off switch

for integrity.

⧽

<small>Pat Croce</small>

Chapter Four

PAR FOR THE COURSE

The ICE model is not rocket science. It is a very simple model—a three-item checklist, easy to remember and incorporate into your thinking as a leader. ICE—integrity, courage, and empathy—is simple but powerful, because if you discipline yourself to reference this model as your leadership compass, you have a much better chance of providing your team with the appropriate direction.

I know this because that is exactly what I have tried to do over the past twenty-plus years in my company. Through many personal experiences I have realized the power of this little recipe. Just think about how effective you could be as a leader if you linked your work ethic and hard-earned competence with decisions and behaviors that were benchmarked against these three critical leadership values—integrity, courage, and empathy.

If each time you had to make a difficult decision, you stopped to do a little examination of your conscience, making sure that your decisions were honest, courageous, and caring, just think how good you would feel and, more important, how well people would respond.

The ICE model is a building-block model that takes leaders from good to great. The first two ingredients, integrity and courage, are absolute essentials. They are must-haves for good leadership, integrity being the foundation of the model. Without it, no one can be a good leader.

If you are dishonest, *then being a good leader is impossible.* In fact, people who are dishonest are not good at anything that makes an important contribution. Those who think of themselves as leaders, yet who lack integrity, live in a haze of denial. They believe that people accept them for who they portray themselves to be, not for who they really are. And that is not so—people can see right through their pretense.

Dishonest leaders rationalize their behavior with the hope that people around them and in their organization buy into their lies, excuses, and thin explanations. But they wear blinders when they do this, and unfortunately for them after a very short period of time they are exposed for the phonies they really are. Sometimes their exposure comes as a surprise. They get so good at rationalizing their behaviors and actions, they start to believe their own spin. They see themselves coasting along very nicely and think that the people they lead actually believe them.

They deceive themselves, however, for in reality the people they lead are busy scheming against them, trying to find ways to undermine them. I have seen it time after time. Once the team figures out that the leader lacks credibility, it is over. Once you provide members of your team with good reasons to doubt your true intentions and second-guess your decisions, your leadership position is a house of cards.

When you were a child, did you ever try building a house of playing cards on the table or the rug? It's fun! But if you've ever built one, you can understand the imagery here. It takes only a little vibration from a breath of air for the house, which took you hours to build, to crumble and fall. What a disappointment!

In the very recent past, we have a number of great examples of this. Our televisions and newspapers have been filled with stories about the trials of dishonest leaders in such notorious houses as Enron, Adelphia, Tyco, Quest, and HealthSouth that crashed because their leaders lacked this simple, critical ingredient—integrity. All it took was a couple of tremors, such as a weak earnings report, a smoking-gun memo, or a disgruntled employee, and the foundation started to shake. The house of cards began to list, and then the aftershocks of cover-ups, lies, and unsupported excuses finished the job. The results were indictments, trials, convictions, losses of billions of dollars in market capitalization, as well as the complete vaporization of employee pensions. Most sadly, tens of thousands of good, committed, hard-working people in these companies suddenly lost their jobs—their primary means of providing for themselves and their families.

Today we have laws like Sarbanes-Oxley (2002) and a plethora of new accounting regulations because corporate officers, the individuals who were entrusted and empowered to lead with integrity, lacked that key value. Some may say those corporate officers were greedy, and others may attribute the demise of these companies to the arrogance of those who led them. I am sure those character flaws were contributing factors, but the real root of the problem was simply this: the leaders of these organizations lacked integrity. They were liars, and arguably they contributed to the financial ruin of thousands upon thousands of employees and investors.

I will bet you that people in leadership positions who lack integrity have also cheated on other important things throughout their lives. As kids they probably cheated on tests. Later in life they probably cheated on their spouses, and they probably cheated everywhere they believed it gave them an advantage. In business, leaders without integrity are the true weapons of mass destruction. Just look at the devastation of Enron. The alleged accounting fraud that took place at Enron cost their shareholders approximately $60 billion in market capitalization. More important, thousands of people who placed their trust in these leaders lost their pensions and jobs.

That is, indeed, mass destruction, a huge mansion of cards falling, but the enemies of Enron were right inside the business, not driving at it with truck bombs from the outside. This is a classic case, really. In the same way, ancient Rome, a huge, powerful empire that stretched from the coast of Spain east to Asia Minor, was weakened first on the inside by lies and corruption before it could be attacked successfully from the outside by tribes to the north.

Several years ago there was a terrific book written about the demise of organized crime in Philadelphia. It was written by a pretty high-ranking mobster who had entered the witness protection program after breaking *omerta*, the code of silence. As a mobster he had made his money on being, among other things, a very effective con artist. His field of expertise was finding dishonest, greedy people and seducing these unsuspecting victims with his phony charm until they let down their guard. Then he knew how to con them out of everything he could get.

He goes into great detail in his book explaining several of his scams and showing how easy it was for him to fool people who were seduced by his slickness and by his get-rich-quick schemes. He took great delight in stealing their fortunes, devastating their businesses, and ruining their lives. One statement he makes, however, is so true and so important for leadership. The mobster concludes that in all his years of working as a con man, one thing was absolutely certain: "You can never con an honest person."

Make no mistake about it: integrity is very straightforward. It concerns telling the truth—no rationalizing, no compromising, no backpedaling, and no justifying. And it starts with being true to oneself. As my dear friend Pat Croce—successful entrepreneur, ex-president of the Philadelphia 76ers, and the best motivational speaker on the planet—likes to say, "There is no on-off switch for integrity."

As leaders we learn to be spinmasters. We are taught to turn lemons into lemonade, and many times that *is* an important part of our jobs. We do this with good intent because we want to keep the morale of our teams high during challenging times. But, as leaders who aim to be true to ourselves, we know deep down inside when we are honestly trying to keep people motivated and engaged and when our words and actions are hollow, insincere, and untrue. We know when we flatter people, and when we go to extremes and lie outright to their faces.

When I took my first job after graduating from St. Joseph's College in 1977, I worked for a state senator named John Sweeney. He told me something that has stuck with me for thirty years. He said, "Always remember that you look in the mirror every day, whether to shave your face, tie your tie, or comb your hair, and there is no escape from the person who is looking back at you." Sweeney's simple yet cogent image reinforces the importance of being truthful to ourselves. We simply cannot fool ourselves.

In addition to being true to ourselves, leaders with integrity must be honest with all the people around them. That does not mean just the people who report to you. It also includes your colleagues and even your bosses.

Leaders with integrity tell the truth, and they do it regardless of the nature of the news—and regardless of who the recipient of the news is. Unfortunately, I have known too many individuals in positions of leadership who are terrific at telling the truth when the news is good. They are the first ones to show up at your office to inform you that you won an award or that your presentation was well done or that you got that promotion you wanted so badly.

Yet these same individuals struggle with bad news, the important constructive criticism that people need in order to grow and develop in their careers. These gladhanders prefer to procrastinate when it comes to addressing difficult, delicate, or distasteful issues. They simply can't handle the task of facing individuals and telling them what they absolutely need to know, because the truth in feedback situations is often unpleasant. So they put it off or they sweep it under the carpet, with the hope that one day it will go away.

They don't understand that bad news is not like good red wine; it does not get better with age. It almost always gets bitter with age.

Two other things about integrity are important to consider and internalize. The first is that in almost all cases, integrity, like time, is not a commodity. Once it is spent, it is gone. We only have so many ticks of the clock or beats of the heart on this planet, and although we like to think we can, it is impossible for us to save time or ever get it back. I suggest that as leaders, we think about integrity in the same precious and valuable way. Once it is spent or exhausted, it becomes extremely difficult, if not impossible, to recapture the trust and reliance of the people you lead. It is almost always gone. Once people doubt your veracity and credibility, it is very hard for them to ever really trust in you again.

Trust is critical in any environment, but to a leader in the business world trust is a key ingredient that effects outcomes and drives results. Effective leaders are adroit at interpersonal relations in two dimensions—vertical and horizontal.

In a vertical relationship, boss to employee, the leader relies on both trust and authority to influence individuals and effect outcomes. In this relationship, trust, of course, is helpful, but when all is said and done, the boss can always utilize his or her authority to make things happen. Clearly, this is the easier relationship to manage. In a horizontal relationship, peer-to-peer (e.g., business-unit leader, general manager), effective leaders must *build* trust *with* their colleagues. As a result, their ability to influence without control enables them to effect change and make things happen. Here, trust catalyzes a leader's ability to influence his or her colleagues.

One example of the role that trust plays in this dynamic is in conflict management, where colleagues have opposing positions on the same issue. Consider two business-unit leaders of equal status who disagree about resource allocation, organizational structure, strategic initiatives, or candidate selection for a key position. In these situations, the discussions will express conflict. There will be compromises and, ultimately, there will be decisions.

As one of the peer leaders, you will not be able simply to will your way through this process. You have no authority over your colleague, and he or she has their own point of view. So only through your ability to influence this decision in a way you believe will be in the organization's best interest will you get the organization to a decision and then to a resolution.

In addition, you should want this to be a productive and positive process, one where you maintain a healthy working relationship with your colleague, where you keep collateral damage to a minimum. Leaving roadkill behind you is not a good resolution because invariably you two will meet again on another issue: you are peers and colleagues, remember?

As you can easily see, if a lack of trust comes between you and your counterpart, then your ability to influence him or her at least to understand your position will be limited. The result may be what you want, but the process will be very messy. For example, it may involve end runs to your boss and backroom politicking with other peers and influential individuals. This negative behavior will result in a downward spiral where trust between you and your peer is further eroded.

Now consider the same situation between two peers who differ on an issue, but who have built up a solid foundation of trust. They have worked to build an interpersonal, horizontal relationship where openness, candor, full transparency, and mutual respect are part of their standard operating procedure.

There are no surprises between these two because they approach conflict by first discussing issues honestly between them. Finally, they operate with an agenda that contemplates the best outcome for the organization before it contemplates their own career advancement. These two leaders will be able to resolve conflicts through influence, and they will continue to foster a trusting relationship that will build upon itself.

I have a relationship just like that with one of my peers at GlaxoSmithKline. His name is Pete Hare, and he is the leader for our HIV business unit. His division is very similar to my Neurohealth division in that Pete's division and my division are relatively small in terms of number of employees, but both divisions make large contributions to the organization's bottom line. Pete's unit has about two hundred people, and my unit has about six hundred. Both HIV and Neurohealth are considered specialty business units, because the medicines we promote are highly scientific and because our targeted customers are exclusively specialists, such as infectious disease doctors and neurologists.

A little history is important here to understand the context of Pete's and my relationship. Prior to GlaxoWellcome's merger with SmithKline, I had responsibility for all the specialty business units in the U.S. business. So in addition to Neurohealth, our Oncology and HIV businesses also reported to me. At that same time, Pete was working at a very senior level inside our Global Commercial Strategy and Development organization. Although I knew his name and I knew a little bit about him, I never had a lot of direct contact with him.

Once the merger occurred, the company decided that we would establish individual and distinct specialty units in the U.S. business. They would no longer be consolidated under one leader. Pete was selected to run the HIV unit; Kevin Lokay, another great guy, was selected to head up the Oncology unit; and I was left with the Neurohealth unit. I provide this background because, as you might imagine, relinquishing a large piece of my current responsibilities to someone else, let alone to someone whom I hardly knew, could present challenges to establishing a trusting horizontal relationship. I could have viewed Pete as a trespasser in my sandbox!

But from day one, none of those challenges materialized. Pete's approach to me was open, candid, and collegial, and thus I was able to reciprocate. Our relationship became one of trust. Although we have differed on issues—some of them pretty significant—we always discussed them first between ourselves so that we knew where each of us stood before we aired them openly with others. Because we had vetted our positions one-on-one, colleague-to-colleague, neither one of us was ever surprised. I never heard anything from our boss or from our respective peers unless I heard it first from Pete. And I am pretty confident that he feels the same way about my behavior. Today, we serve as mentors for each other, discussing everything from company strategy to our own personal development, even internal and external career opportunities, because we have a relationship built on complete trust and high integrity.

Quite frankly, I wish all of my relationships with other people in leadership positions were as trusting as the one that Pete and I share. Unfortunately, all of them are not at the same level. In some situations I have been surprised on issues of personnel, resource allocation, or even organizational structure, all of which would have significant impacts on my business, simply because someone did the old end run. No open, candid, and transparent conversations with me took place first. And where they did not, those situations left me angry and frustrated. Most important, they compromised my trust in the people who operated in that manner.

Another absolute tenet is that there are no degrees of integrity. It is a zero-sum game. You either tell the truth in its entirety or you are lying. Again, Pat Croce is correct: "There is no on-off switch for integrity."

A sentence that has crept into our company jargon since our recent merger with SmithKline is, "Does this pass the red-face test?" I absolutely despise it! Whenever I hear it, which is way too often, it is like scratching fingernails across a blackboard. It makes my blood run cold. The implied message in that question is that there are levels or degrees of truth.

How can anyone accept the idea that there are scores for integrity? Does being 70 percent truthful mean you pass the honesty test? I wonder, how much blood must flow into the capillaries of one's face before one fails the integrity test? If there *is* such a thing as an integrity test—and I believe there is—it does not contemplate levels or degrees of truth. It's simple. Any integrity test must be graded either pass or fail. Either something is the truth or it isn't. There is nothing in between. If it is a test for integrity, then by definition it must be a true-false test.

It's obvious that being true to oneself and communicating the truth to those we lead are must-haves. If you peel the "integrity onion" one more layer, however, another test of integrity appears. This integrity test challenges the leader one layer more deeply about how honest they truly are; thus, it is much more difficult to pass.

It requires that you, the leader, always place your team's and your organization's agenda before your own agenda. For leaders with integrity, the needs, time, and activities of the people you lead and the company you represent must always be more important than your own needs, time, and activities. Let me share a story with you that illustrates well the idea that leaders with integrity place the team's agenda before their own agenda. These events really tested my integrity!

It's always easy to preach to your people about what's right to do. The hard part, the challenge, is living it through your own example. This is not a story about a multibillion-dollar deal or some major organizational decision. It is a simple story about seeing what is wrong and what is right and then having to decide what to do.

A couple of years ago, I received a phone call from one of our procurement directors. This person was responsible for buying television, radio, and print space for all of our direct-to-consumer advertisements. In our business we call that "DTC." (I admit, we use a lot of acronyms.)

Unless you have been in hibernation for the past ten years, you probably know that today almost all major U.S. pharmaceutical companies spend millions of dollars annually advertising prescription medicines on network television, through radio broadcasts, and in popular magazines and daily newspapers. It is almost impossible to watch prime-time television without seeing some commercial about the newest prescription medicine to relieve your high cholesterol, asthma, or hay fever, or to reduce your blood pressure.

The intent is to get prospective patients who are the consumers of our medicines to recognize the symptoms of a particular disease they or a family member might have, and then to associate the brand name of the sponsoring company's medicine with their disease. Our goal in using direct-to-consumer advertising is to get the end user or patient to engage in meaningful conversation with his or her physician. Ultimately we want that prospective customer to walk into the doctor's office and request a medicine by its brand name. Probably the most notorious example of this approach has been Pfizer's promotion of Viagra for erectile dysfunction. The lasting imprint on the viewer's mind is of some middle-aged celebrity or chiseled athlete telling consumers how the little blue pill helped rejuvenate their sex lives.

The bottom line is that these ads work very effectively. In addition, the TV networks, radio stations, and print publications love our lucrative sponsorships. And quite frankly, these ads serve a purpose beyond increasing awareness for the advertised medicine. From a public service perspective, they destigmatize diseases by bringing the more personal ones into the marketplace, by empowering patients to become more educated about medicines available to treat their illnesses and conditions, and by showing them how to grow more comfortable discussing sensitive issues with their health-care providers.

One of the big-name publications, then, with whom we did a lot of DTC business, placing ads for our various medicines, contacted one of our people in procurement with an invitation. They wanted one of our senior executives to join their board members for a brief advisory meeting that also included two rounds of golf, dinner, and one night's sleeping accommodations. This was not an unusual request. Several of our suppliers would often set up meetings such as these with our senior people to ensure that they were meeting our expectations and to build better business relationships.

The only problem, though, was the location for this advisory meeting—Augusta, Georgia. The golf would be played on the same course that hosts the Masters Championship, and the sleeping accommodations would be in Augusta National's own Eisenhower Cabin. If you know anything about Augusta National, you know that playing this course and sleeping in the Eisenhower Cabin is the dream of every avid golfer. Knowing full well that I am an avid golfer, our director of procurement contacted me with this once-in-a-lifetime invitation.

At first I was excited, and my instinctive response was to accept. Oh, yes! It didn't take long, though, for me to become really conflicted. On the one hand, there could be no better perk than to play Augusta National, not to mention sleeping and dining there.

As a kid I had fallen totally in love with the game of golf. For me the Masters always signaled the beginning of golf season. Just like the first whiff of burning leaves during football season and the first sound of cracking bats during baseball season, Masters weekend was a signal that golf would blossom just like the gorgeous azaleas and dogwoods that frame Augusta National. It was time to dust off my treasured Sam Snead Blue Ridge irons, pull out a couple of old shag balls, and head to the nearest vacant field to get the rust off my swing and prepare for a wonderful summer of golf. So the Masters created a very memorable vision in my mind dating back to my first days of playing the game.

Several years ago, I actually had the privilege of attending a Masters tournament, and I can assure you that Augusta National is every bit as beautiful a golf course as one might imagine. Oddly enough, the course sits in this little nondescript southern town. You would never expect the world's most beautiful eighteen holes of golf to be located in this dusty, bland town of strip malls and fast-food restaurants. Augusta National is truly a diamond in the rough, founded by the legendary Bobby Jones, a Georgia native and one of the greatest amateur golfers in the history of the game.

Once you walk down Magnolia Lane and onto the hallowed grounds of the Augusta National golf course, everything changes dramatically, in a split second. The landscape morphs right before your eyes, just like what happens when Dorothy walks into Oz. Tire stores and burger joints baking in the sun turn into a green, flowered expanse, indescribably beautiful. Everything about Augusta National is more pronounced than you can imagine. The grass is greener. The hills are steeper. The dogwoods and the azaleas are radiant with pink, red, and white light. The clubhouse is prouder than what you would have expected to see. It is simply spectacular.

Needless to say, when I received the invitation, I was chomp-
ing at the bit to go. On the other hand, I had a feeling gnawing
inside of me that just did not feel right. My conscience, that little
Jiminy Cricket from *Pinocchio*, kept questioning my judgment
and reminding me to "let your conscience be your guide." I kept
thinking about looking at myself in the mirror, as John Sweeney
had told me. I knew this was an integrity challenge.

But I was certain that I could rationalize my way around corporate policy. I knew I could make a case, albeit a weak one, that
it was perfectly okay to take three days out of my busy schedule,
one for travel and two for golf. It would strengthen a good business
relationship for me, on behalf of Glaxo, to hang out with folks
from a publication where we spend millions of dollars in advertising...and to facilitate this valuable relationship at a meeting site
with the most revered eighteen holes of golf in the world.

The devil on my left shoulder was shouting, "Do it! Everybody
does it," but the angel on my right shoulder was whispering,
"Don't do it, Steve. You know this isn't right," and quite frankly
the angel was whispering everything I really didn't want to hear.

These urgent whispers were also a reminder that you lead with
integrity only when you practice the same honesty standards that
you profess to others and especially to those you lead. Yes, it was
about being true to myself, but more important it was about being
an example to those who report to me, and it was about agendas.
Was my personal agenda going to supersede the agendas of the
people I lead? Was I being selfish? In this case, if I went on the
trip, the message was clear—my personal agenda was clearly more
important than my team's agenda.

I would be taking three days where sun, fun, food, beer, golf, and the incredibly seductive attraction of Augusta National would be more important to me than the mundane yet important business issues that my group would be addressing. Let's face it, I would be out of pocket for three days. How many important phone calls would I miss and need to return? How many business issues would have to wait until I was done cleaning the grooves from my clubs or taking a bite from another cucumber sandwich? More important, deep down inside, the most gnawing problem was that I knew there was no real business need for me to be there.

So I made a tough decision. I knew that I would probably never get another chance like this. But I also knew that seventy-two hours of euphoria at Augusta would be followed by what would seem like an eternity of guilt.

This one was a true moral test for me. I really wanted to go, and I was so tortured that I still struggled even after I discerned the right thing to do. I mean I really struggled. I kept asking people around me if they thought it would be okay to go to Augusta. I was looking for a misery-loves-company companion, someone who loved golf and who could understand my misery if I didn't get to go, someone who would convince me that what I wanted to do was okay.

Finally, after days of stewing, I decided not to go. I called our procurement director and said, "I want you to know how much I appreciate the offer, but I do not feel that I can go." He sounded a little perplexed but said he understood and would let the publishing company know that I had declined their invitation.

When I heard those three words, "declined their invitation,"

I felt a chill because I knew there was no going back. That was the end of the dream, the beginning of the waking world, and I would have to live with it. Many times now I daydream about that possible experience, especially when I am on a golf course and someone asks, "Did you ever play Augusta National"?

But in retrospect, I have no regrets. As I said, playing Augusta National would have been the opportunity of a lifetime. As it turned out, even though I struggled with the decision, with that pain-in-the-ass angel on one shoulder reminding me of the importance of leading with integrity and that golf-loving devil on the other shoulder describing the beauty of Amen Corner, I made the right call.

That call fortifies me with the license, the credibility to push others in our organization to demonstrate integrity by putting the agendas of the teams they lead before their own agenda. It was a call to prioritize my values, and it reinforced my first boss's image of looking at myself honestly in the mirror every day.

I tell this story, however, not to polish my integrity halo. Nothing could be further from the truth. I just want to illustrate the challenge of putting your team's agenda before your own agenda. The truth is I tried as hard as I could to justify going to Augusta. I really struggled with the decision. My passion to play golf anywhere, let alone Augusta, and actually spend a night in the historic Eisenhower Cabin was so strongly alluring that it almost overcame my belief in being true to myself and being honest with my team. It would have been so cool, so sexy, to go on that trip. Just think of the great, rich stories I could have told my golfing buddies!

But integrity is not about being cool or sexy. It's about making difficult decisions and doing what is right—*that* was the opportunity of a lifetime. That experience gave me the chance to take on a tough challenge and to step up. I don't for a minute regret my decision to decline the trip—well, maybe for a minute or two every year during Masters week!

In 1972–74, our country was embroiled in the scandal of Watergate. The entire plot and aftermath was a case study in the type of integrity void that screams for placing personal agendas ahead of the team's agenda. In this case, the team was much larger and way more important than my division at GSK; it comprised the citizens of the United States.

Very competent, very experienced public figures like John Mitchell, John Erlichman, H. R. Haldeman, Jeb Stewart McGruder, John Dean, G. Gordon Liddy, and even President Richard Nixon not only lost their powerful jobs, they also lost the trust and confidence of the people they served. In disgrace, some served jail time, and worst of all each of them compromised the trust of the American public. Their actions showed that they valued their own agendas as their most important priority. There is no question that these individuals knew their jobs and understood what it took to lead our country. The problem was that they lacked an essential leadership value, integrity, and it did not take long—in Nixon's case, just fourteen months—for the house of cards to crumble.

What was it that caused each of these long-serving public servants to compromise their integrity? They were well-known, prestigious, celebrated public figures. They had made important if not historic names for themselves, which they could later turn into millions of dollars in their private careers to follow, and there was no question that Nixon would win reelection in 1972. So why risk it all? Why gamble away careers, years of service, honor, and even public trust?

The prize, the pot of gold at the end of the rainbow, was power and control. It was the ability not only to win the presidency and control the Executive Office, but also to control the legislative branch. If successful, the Watergate break-in would provide important information that would decimate the already weakened Democratic Party. The '72 election would be a Republican landslide, both for the Executive Office and for Congress. In this way, Nixon and his cronies would control and possibly dictate the country's agenda for years to come. That is what Watergate was all about. It was about leaders placing their own agendas before the agenda of the team, of the nation. Theirs was a dishonesty fueled by arrogance, ambition, and the priority of personal agendas.

John Dean, special counsel to President Nixon, wrote a book about it, *Blind Ambition: The White House Years* (1976), and it speaks volumes about how dangerous uncontrolled ambition can be. If you play out the analogy that leaders who lack integrity are the most insidious weapons of mass destruction, then blind ambition is the nuclear seed, the enriching uranium that makes those weapons so powerful and destructive.

In the business world, and especially in the corporate world, it is important to identify leaders whose blind ambition compels them to make poor, parochial, self-serving decisions. They are often the smooth-talking highfliers who make decisions primarily to feather their own nest and to move their careers to higher levels. The earlier you identify these individuals among your team members, the better it is for you, for your team, and for your organization. These selfish leaders need to be exposed and disarmed before the destruction occurs.

On the other hand, it is even more important to identify those real leaders who understand the importance of promoting the team's agenda. These leaders may on the surface appear to be less charismatic and spectacular. They may present a lower public image. They may avoid the limelight, yet they absolutely know their business, and they demonstrate solid values. These leaders get it! They realize that in a high tide, all ships rise, and they are committed to the agenda of the team and the organization before their own agendas.

Since these leaders are unencumbered by personal growth development and self-serving needs, their decisions are liberated from a personal agenda. These leaders truly understand the value of integrity, and they add a very valuable ingredient to their companies: organizational stewardship. Leaders with integrity inspire their teams to performance measures and professional rewards well beyond expectations, and they model organizational stewardship.

Their people can sense the leader's values through their actions as they put the team's and the organization's agenda first and their own agenda second. The team members can look for simple signals, such as how the leader plans his or her day, how they plan their travel, whether they keep their appointments, and whether they live by the same rules they profess to believe.

And make no mistake about it, the people you lead watch you and judge you, and they talk to each other. They draw conclusions based not on your words but on your actions. If you walk the talk, they will follow. Otherwise, they have no options except to fight you, sabotage you, or leave.

The last thing I want to say about integrity is to ask you to think about the unspoken covenant between leaders and followers. That covenant is the same regardless of the work setting. It doesn't matter whether you are in business, the military, sports, education, law, the arts, entertainment, the church, the family, or community service. The implied understanding between leaders and followers goes like this: the people you lead promise to listen, follow directions, work together, and work hard if and only if their leader promises to give direction, provide resources, and lead with honest intent.

The ultimate measure of a man is not where he stands in moments of comfort and convenience but where he stands at times of challenge and controversy.

MARTIN LUTHER KING JR.

Chapter Five

———

KING OF THE FOREST

One of my favorite movies of all time is, believe it or not, *The Wizard of Oz*. From the first time I saw it at the age of five, I was mesmerized, and even today I have to say I love it and never get tired of it. I must own at least three or four copies in both VHS and disc format. I watch it anywhere or any time I want. Occasionally I watch it on regular television, even with commercials! The movie has a wonderful story with some important messages, and I believe it has applications to today's business world.

Its parallels to the challenges of the business environment are many and are helpful to consider. You just need to use your imagination. It is a classic literary setup with a protagonist and an antagonist; from a business perspective, that's like two competing organizations, both of which are led by dynamic leaders. One is led by pigtailed Dorothy Gale, the Kansas girl in a gingham dress. The other is led by the Wicked Witch of the West, dressed in black and sporting a greenish complexion. The Witch's organization consists of the flying monkeys and the sentinels, the ones who chant, "O-Ee-Yah! Eoh-Ah!" Dorothy's organization, on the other hand, is an eclectic cast of characters—the Tin Man, the Scarecrow, and my favorite, the Cowardly Lion.

Dorothy actually leads a line of direct reports with very complementary skills. There is a common currency, the ruby red slippers. Dorothy is warned that the Witch wants those slippers badly because without them she is powerless, and she is also informed that the slippers have a special power and ability to help her realize her own aspirations. There are external stakeholders. For example, Glinda, the Good Witch of the North, knows that if Dorothy prevails and her nemesis the West Witch falls, then she controls all of Munchkin Land in the South. And finally there are the goals, like getting to Oz, and getting the broomstick of the Wicked Witch.

Along the way there are ups and downs for Dorothy and her team. They are in a fiercely competitive battle against the Witch and her team. At first, they make great progress. They are moving down the yellow brick road very nicely when the Witch casts her poppy spell, and suddenly they fall asleep. They lose traction and they lose time. Once they wake up, Dorothy et al. regroup and move on.

They get to Oz, where they are refreshed; then they formulate their plan. But they hit another obstacle when Dorothy and her dog, Toto, are kidnapped by the flying monkeys. The Tin Man, Scarecrow, and Lion now must figure out a way to get inside the Witch's castle and free Dorothy, but before they do that they must first get past those damn annoying monkeys.

All of this parallels developing and implementing strategy in business. In any dynamic market, where the landscape and the challenges keep changing, blueprints for strategy are worthless. I was taught a long time ago by a very smart strategic thinker, Tom Mullen, CEO of a very successful, privately held consulting company, Park Li, that strategy in a dynamic market must be fluid and iterative. That is exactly what Dorothy's team does. Each time there is a change in the landscape or some external event occurs, the four huddle up and call some plays. If they had stuck only to their original game plan, the happy outcome might have been a very different one.

As everyone knows, Dorothy's team prevails. They get inside the Witch's castle and with a little luck they destroy the Witch and retrieve her broomstick. Who knew that water would melt the Witch? That *was* luck! Even with the best, most fluid plans, the best people, and compelling products or services, many times it takes a little luck to realize success and to prevail in the marketplace.

The Cowardly Lion, played by Bert Lahr in the film, is without doubt my favorite character. In my opinion, he steals the show. First of all, he has a good, dry sense of humor, and his timing as well as the delivery of his lines is perfect. Some of his comebacks are absolutely hysterical! He is charming, self-deprecating, and has this unrelenting desire to find the courage that will give him his rightful place in the animal kingdom—king of the forest.

Courage—that desired quality that Bert Lahr's character in this 1939 film classic wanted so badly—is the second critical component of the ICE model and one that is also necessary for good leadership. Like integrity, courage is a must-have value. You can't lead a team if you lack courage.

Courage in leadership starts with having the intestinal fortitude to make difficult decisions in challenging situations. Harry
Truman said after deciding to end World War II with the tragic
destruction of two Japanese cities by atomic bombs and the loss
of millions of lives that he got paid to make the 51-49 percent
decisions. In other words, he was responsible for the close calls,
the tough ones where there were no easy answers but tons of
accountability. That's courage in action.

Truman, who inherited the presidency and the challenge to
end World War II upon the death of Franklin Roosevelt in April
1945, was remembered for two famous comments. Both these
statements demonstrate his belief in the importance of courage
in leadership. Regardless of whether you agree or disagree with
Harry's politics and his decisions, it's difficult to question his
courage as a leader when you know he followed through on "The
buck stops here" and "If you can't stand the heat, get out of the
kitchen." That's courage speaking.

The explosive growth of Glaxo during the 1980s is a business
case study in terms of a very courageous decision. This decision
enabled the company to expand from a relatively unknown
research pharmaceutical company with very little commercial
presence outside Europe to a fully integrated commercial giant in
today's worldwide pharmaceutical industry. Amazingly, all of this
happened in about five years, from 1978 to 1983, and most of it
was due primarily to one person who had the courage to make, as
Truman would say, "a 51-49 percent decision."

Prior to the end of the 1970s, Glaxo's modest success in the
pharmaceutical industry was due to its productive research labs

and its conservative commercialization of the medicines discovered in those labs. The company's approach was to research and develop new and effective medicines in highly prevalent disease areas familiar to Glaxo's scientists. These included disease areas like asthma, inflammatory skin disease (psoriasis, eczema, etc.), and infection. Glaxo's core capability was to identify targets in the body associated with those diseases and to find medicines to fit those targets. Glaxo was effective with this scientific approach, called receptor-chemistry technology, and their research labs were productive in producing very good medicines. Glaxo would then market their medicines themselves in countries where they had a strong commercial foothold, such as England, Italy, and India, but they would also out-license those same medicines to pharmaceutical companies in other markets throughout the world, where they had little or no commercial presence. In return, Glaxo would realize a small but predictable royalty payment.

Thus, popular medicines that were major sellers in large commercial markets like the United States—products such as Keflex, for bacterial infections, a Glaxo-researched product—had been commercialized there by Eli Lilly. Other well-known medicines, like Vanceril for asthma and Valisone for psoriasis, were also researched and developed in Glaxo's labs. But they, too, were commercialized in the United States by another pharmaceutical company, Schering, which was licensed by Glaxo to sell those medicines there.

All of that, however, was about to change when Glaxo's labs produced another new advancement in medicine called ranitidine (the brand became known as Zantac). Zantac would help change the way doctors treated acid-related ailments such as stomach ulcers and gastroesophageal reflux disease, otherwise known as heartburn. Up until the availability of Zantac, patients with stomach ulcers or other acid-related diseases had three medical choices—surgery, antacids (such as Maalox), or Tagamet, a product that works in a similar way to Zantac.

Tagamet, like Zantac, belongs to a class of drugs called histamine receptor antagonists. They work by blocking those histamine receptors in the gastrointestinal tract that are responsible for the production of stomach acid, or hydrochloric acid. When too much hydrochloric acid is secreted, the result is a burning feeling in the stomach or the esophagus. Just eat a pepperoni pizza and drink a beer or two right before bedtime and you probably will experience a nice case of gastroesophageal reflux—lots of stomach acid and burning pain! Tagamet was the first of its class on the market. Zantac was the second market entrant, and we believed it offered clinical features and benefits that could differentiate Zantac in a positive way from Tagamet. In clinical trials it appeared as though Zantac lacked some of the side effects like impotence and mental confusion that doctors saw becoming more prevalent with Tagamet. And from a potency perspective arguably Zantac lasted longer, so it needed to be taken fewer times per day than the existing form of Tagamet.

Not only did Zantac change the way doctors treated these ailments, it also changed the way Glaxo would commercialize products from that time until today. Zantac became a real commercial litmus test for Glaxo. The challenge was that Zantac was just too big a commercial opportunity to allow other companies to realize the lion's share of revenues and profits in rich markets like the United States. The stomach ulcer and hypersecretory market were huge opportunities, and the medical need was wide open. This market dwarfed other therapeutic areas like asthma and skin disorders. Zantac was a home run looking for a ballpark!

But many on the board at Glaxo PLC were very comfortable with their current out-licensing strategy. Their approach had worked for years; they were so complacent with this strategy that they were planning to do it again with Zantac. The company was in serious negotiations with the world's largest pharmaceutical company, Merck, to out-license the United States rights for Zantac to them. Then it happened: a critical, difficult, and courageous decision was made by our chief financial officer, Paul Gerolomi.

Gerolomi, also a board member, believed that Glaxo needed to take on the responsibility of commercializing Zantac in all markets throughout the world. He was convinced that out-licensing Zantac in profitable markets like Europe and the United States would be a big mistake. He believed that Glaxo needed to build and establish sales and marketing operations in markets where we previously had had little commercial presence so that we could reap the full rewards of this highly profitable medicine and so that we could optimize the full potential of profitable medicines percolating in Glaxo's lab.

His first priority was the United States, easily the richest pharmaceutical market in the world. So with Sir Paul's vision, direction, and support, Glaxo purchased a small, privately held pharmaceutical company, Meyer Laboratories, in Fort Lauderdale, Florida. From that base, Gerolomi hoped that Glaxo could expand its presence in the United States and become a major player in the global pharmaceutical industry. This acquisition process began in 1978. By November 1980, Glaxo severed the Zantac deal with Merck, and by July 1983, Zantac was launched by Glaxo in the United States.

We were small, but we were a very proud and hungry commercial team. With five more years of hard work and very savvy commercial tactics, we propelled Zantac into the *Guinness Book of World Records* (1988) as the first medicine ever to reach $1 billion in sales in the U.S. market. And by 1989 Paul Gerolomi, that little, unassuming chief financial officer with the courage of a lion, became Sir Paul Gerolomi, the knight and chairman of the board of Glaxo PLC, and, I might add, king of the forest.

Courage in leadership, though, goes well beyond the Truman model or the Gerolomi story of making tough decisions. Courage is also about having sufficient confidence in oneself to trust your team to perform. In other words, having courage means empowering the team's members with the freedom to perform to the best of their ability and to make an important impact on the success of the organization.

Really, all people need from courageous leaders is vision, guidance, and support for them to do their jobs effectively. They want the leader's ability and confidence to create a productive environment. But it takes courage, a lot of courage, to entrust and liberate people to perform. You have to step back and avoid the temptation to micromanage, and then you have to support the decisions and actions that the team makes. It sounds easy, but it is tough to do. I can assure you that for me this is the toughest part of leading with courage—letting go and stepping back.

I cannot tell you how many times I have heard people in leadership positions say something like this to their staff: "Okay, you can go ahead with that decision, but I'm not sure that I support it." I have heard that line or variations on it hundreds of times in my career, and each time it created the same blood-curdling feeling in me. I can't believe anyone in leadership would say, "Go ahead, but I don't support it." It's just so lame, so weak, so cowardly. Imagine being in a situation where your team is making a tough call and you give them that kind of tepid support. Do you really think they feel empowered to move forward, take on challenges, then succeed when you give and take back in the same breath? Who would sign up to get in formation behind *that* guy?

In 2001, shortly after our merger with SmithKline, I was given the opportunity to lead a cross-functional team on a very, very important GlaxoSmithKline project. This project would prove to be an excellent chance for me to practice the value of demonstrating courage by empowering a team to perform.

I had just completed four days in a leadership program in the south of France. I am not real fond of traveling anywhere, especially outside the safe borders of the United States, but actually this turned out to be a very good experience. Our chief executive officer, Jean-Pierre Garnier, or J.P. as he is fondly known, had convened about forty or fifty people in various leadership positions to address key business issues. He would utilize this program as an opportunity to generate healthy, critical thinking around challenges and opportunities that he would be addressing, as well as a chance for the participants in the program to network with their colleagues around the world, colleagues we would otherwise not get to know. Actually, it's a very good program.

On the final day I was in my room anxiously packing my bags to go home when I got a call from David Stout, who at the time was president of GSK's U.S. business. He reported to J.P., and I reported to him. During our conversation, he shared with me his concern that our industry and our company were getting beaten up by the press and politicians because of the costs of prescription medicines, primarily the high costs to the elderly population.

Generally, David was referring to seniors in the Medicare program and disabled people who did not have access to a funded program for prescription medicines. Unbelievable as it may seem, at that time many of those who consume the most medicines—the elderly—had no means of payment except out of pocket, so as David said, it was very easy for politicians and newscasters to place blame on the pharmaceutical companies for creating this crisis. It was perceived that through our "greed," the high cost of prescription medicines caused the elderly to make choices between medicines and other necessities.

The press and, of course, the politicians were having a field day with this. It was just so easy to make us look bad. Politicians love to identify and attack a villain to get votes, and the press also loves to attack an easy mark to sell more newspapers. Conveniently, the representatives, senators, and press failed to tell the public that our country's own law was culpable. Medicare, the law passed in 1965, never included coverage for outpatient prescription medicines. It covered doctor visits and hospitalizations and medicines dispensed in hospitals, but it did not reimburse for most medicines dispensed through the neighborhood pharmacy. You see, then, our own lawmakers had failed to provide prescription drug coverage for the elderly where it was needed the most.

Unless you were lucky enough to belong to an employer-sponsored retiree program that included outpatient prescription drug coverage, you were simply out of luck. So the majority of the 40-plus million elderly, those citizens over sixty-five years old and other Medicare-eligible disabled persons, had no prescription drug coverage. They had to pay cash, whereas almost everyone else had some kind of third-party coverage for prescription medicines. This was a political and public-relations tornado, and our industry was right in the path of the storm.

David knew that we were beginning to feel battered by the winds. The press and the politicians were characterizing us as egregious profiteers, when clearly it was the governmental system that was at fault. My boss, David Stout, wanted a solution. He wanted GlaxoSmithKline to step up and offer something that would help patients, something that would help to show that GlaxoSmith-Kline was the kind of company that tried to solve a big problem for this elderly population.

If you work for many years in any organization as I have, you are certain to experience opportunities that excite your competitive juices and test your ability to lead. Most times, however, leadership and inspiration are practiced during day-to-day, routine activities, such as budget reviews, making and carrying out tactical plans, and personnel development. The things you do on a daily basis are critical challenges of leadership stamina. Folks in the organization want to see leadership staying power, and they want to see it with consistency. But every once in a while you get the chance to demonstrate special leadership by directing and empowering a team taking on a key initiative that will have a significant impact on your organization or even the industry in which you work.

That is exactly what happened to me with the Orange Card initiative. This was a special chance for me to lead a team that would really make an impact on our company and on our industry. More importantly, it was an opportunity to make a large impact on the lives of millions of patients.

The credibility of our industry was on the line. Our public relations score had dipped below the score for the oil companies in the 1970s, and we were only a few points above the big tobacco companies. Imagine that! An industry that spends tens of billions of dollars every year on research to find medicines that improve, extend, or even save people's lives was viewed almost as badly as an industry that markets nicotine, what C. Everett Koop, our former surgeon general and "America's Doctor," referred to as the most addictive drug known to man. That is how badly the perception of the U.S. research-based pharmaceutical industry had fallen. It was a mind-boggling nightmare but it was true—the public was, as they said in the 1970s Oscar-winning movie *Network*, "mad as hell and they were not going to take it anymore."

During this time, our company was also going through a big change. In January 2001, two pharmaceutical giants, GlaxoWellcome and SmithKline Beecham, had come together and merged into one mega-company, GlaxoSmithKline. These were not just any two companies. These were two fiercely competitive companies that, for the past fifteen years, had gone head-to-head against each other in a number of substantially valuable therapeutic categories, like ulcers, infections, and nausea. There was no love lost between them. Additionally, the two organizational cultures were vastly different.

Needless to say, by July of that year, there was quite a bit of chaos at GSK. Our industry was under a lot of public relations pressure, and our new company was feeling the heat, confusion, and frustration of a merger.

The Orange Card initiative was, then, just what the doctor ordered to address both our external image challenge and our internal merger challenge. The Orange Card was designed so participants could realize average savings of 30 percent off the usual price they paid for outpatient GSK medicines. In some cases, those savings could be 40 percent or greater, depending on the pharmacy's usual and customary price for the prescribed GSK medicine.

The Orange Card initiative was a chance for us to put ICE into action. Let's break it apart and look at each component of the model. Integrity—it was absolutely the right thing to do. It was GlaxoSmithKline putting the public's health-care agenda before its own corporate, financial agenda. We did no analysis of profit and loss. We would do it regardless of the financial implications. We had committed to the concept that this program was going to provide a 30–40 percent discount to people who had previously paid full sticker price for our medicines.

Courage—GlaxoSmithKline was going to step out on its own, making a move that would catch the rest of the industry by surprise.

Antitrust laws prevent companies from getting together to decide how they will price products, so this very bold move had to be made alone. We had to have the intestinal fortitude to discount in a market where very few companies had discounted before.

Empathy—we put ourselves in the shoes of our customers, those senior citizens who had no coverage for prescription medicines, and we put ourselves in the shoes of the people in our organization. We knew that a feeling of pride would permeate the new team of GlaxoSmithKline when we became recognized as the company to step up to the plate and offer a solution to this problem. This bold initiative would unite and catalyze our newly formed team—GSK.

As I mentioned before, the challenge to make this happen was given to me by David Stout, president of GlaxoSmithKline, U.S. I would be remiss if I did not recognize the team of people who actually did the work to put this program on the market. There was Diane Tulp, a vice president in our commercial organization, and Robin White, who worked for Diane; Mary Ann Rhyne and Julie Dean, who handled our public relations; Bill Leonard, Kim Crutchfield, John Cheppo-McCormick, Jim Tallet, and Jim Williams from our Managed Care Department; Sally Walsh and Janie Kinney from our Washington office; and Bill Edwards from our Legal Department. Each one of these individuals, in addition to carrying out his or her daily responsibilities, worked diligently on this project.

By September 2001, we had a program ready to introduce into the market that would provide eligible Medicare patients with a real-time discount, right at the pharmacy counter, for all GlaxoSmithKline medicines. No need for paperwork or filling out forms by the elderly! It was as simple as this. They just handed the pharmacist their prescription along with what we called the GSK Orange Card and the discount would be applied electronically at the time the medicine was being dispensed. It only took us three months to take this program from conception to inception.

We had, however, one unfortunate time problem. The day before we intended to introduce the Orange Card was September 11, the same day two jets crashed into the towers of the World Trade Center in New York; the same day one jet crashed into the Pentagon; the same day United Flight 93, which was intended to crash into the White House, was taken down by its heroic passengers outside of Pittsburgh.

Needless to say, we had to postpone the launch of the Orange Card until a later date. We caught a period of time that was perfect: early November 2001 and, as Bill Leonard said later, "It was kind of a break in the weather"—right between the tragedy of September 11 and the U.S. invasion of Afghanistan. The Orange Card became a very welcome and newsworthy announcement. We introduced it on Capitol Hill in the presence of Secretary of Health Tommy Thompson, along with a large contingent of Pennsylvania and North Carolina senators and congresspersons because GSK has two locations for its U.S. operations, both very large. One is in North Carolina, and the other one is in Pennsylvania.

Newspapers, television, and radio stations from across the country covered the story. It was big news, and it did not take long before other pharmaceutical companies copied the Orange Card by introducing cards or programs of their own for this population of patients. We believe the Orange Card led the way for the creation of these other industry initiatives for savings programs, eventually resulting in a program called Together Rx—a one-card program for six to seven companies. Ultimately, the Orange Card catalyzed the passage of what exists today. Today we have a funded Medicare Prescription Drug Benefit; although it is long overdue, we now have one, and I believe the Orange Card played an important role in making that happen. The passage of The Medicare Modernization Act now provides a funded pharmaceutical benefit for senior citizens, and it's about time!!

Courage is not just needed for making tough decisions. It is also vital for trusting and empowering teams to do their best work—giving them the direction, resources, and support they need to get the job done without imposing the shackles of micromanagement. That is what we did. In developing the Orange Card, we never micromanaged the team or the process. We gave them the direction, support, resources, and encouragement they needed. Then we got out of their way so that they could figure out what had to be done and how to do it. That is why we were able to get the Orange Card into the market within three months of conception.

Finally, courage is also about rewards and recognition. Courageous leaders allow the members of a team to bask in the glory of success whenever they have a successful experience; by the same token, courageous leaders also shoulder the responsibility whenever the experience does not go as expected. In this way, the team is liberated to think and act creatively. That is what we did with the Orange Card. It was a resounding success, so it was our responsibility to make sure that each team member was rewarded financially and recognized publicly for his or her contributions.

Three things enabled GSK to introduce the Orange Card successfully and allowed us to polish our tarnished halo. First, make no mistake about it, was David Stout's courage and vision, just like that of Sir Paul Gerolomi, to create a GSK solution. Second was our assembling an effective cross-functional team to make decisions and take action, and finally it was our courage to empower the team to do its work, support the team's decisions, and reward them for their fine performance.

It is simple. The team was successful and the mission was completed because we demonstrated the type of courage that enabled them to realize the freedom of empowerment, the inspiration of achievement, and the benefits of reward and recognition.

Right after the launch of the Orange Card, I held a celebration party at my house. Each team member as well as their spouse or guest was invited, and so were all the senior executives at GSK. It was a wonderful evening! GSK's executives, such as Bob Ingram, our chief operating officer and an icon in the pharmaceutical industry; Mike Corrigan, our chief financial officer; Anna McClafferty and Katheryn O'Fee, colleagues of mine on our Operating Committee; Tom Kaney, head of human resources; and, of course, our president, David Stout, the person who had the initial idea for GSK to do something to help Medicare patients, were present. The team was ecstatic about the recognition they received. Our executives made sure that they knew how much we appreciated what they had accomplished. It was truly an opportunity to allow them to bask in the glory of their success.

At this party I unexpectedly met someone who would have a dramatic impact on me professionally and who would also play a key role in helping me formulate and communicate the ICE model. Karol Wasylyshn is an organizational psychologist. I have no idea what organizational psychologists do, and I am not sure I *want* to know, but I do know that Karol has coached many senior executives in the business world and at SmithKline. She is chief executive of her own company and is also a practicing psychologist. Her specialty is executive coaching. Karol is a believer in the importance of leadership values, effective organizational culture, and emotional intelligence.

She believes and teaches that how leaders operate is just as important as what leaders accomplish. Today that may seem abnormal because we are so focused on results. To me, however, her approach is a breath of fresh air; I see plenty of proof in the literature that validates beyond a doubt the idea that leaders who have a high EQ (emotional intelligence quotient) create the most value for their companies. Chief executive officers who understand the emotional elements of leadership are more likely to create a working environment that is collaborative and collegial. In addition, time after time leaders with high emotional intelligence are much more likely to create more shareholder value. Karol is an absolute crusader about the importance of emotional intelligence and holding organizational values in collaborative leadership.

I was fortunate to run into her at our party. She was a guest of our head of human resources, Tom Kaney. As luck would have it, we struck up a conversation and there was an instant connection:

Karol and I were on the same page of the hymnal. I could not believe it. It was so refreshing to talk with someone, who, just like me, believes so strongly in what others might call the soft stuff in business. She was also into leadership skills like collaborative culture and leader visibility, approachability, and humility.

Think about it: once the Wizard of Oz has given the Tin Man a heart, the Scarecrow a brain, and the Cowardly Lion courage, Dorothy's team collaborates well to accomplish her mighty goal—to return home to Kansas. No more losing traction and time in whining, self-pity, or sleeping in the poppy fields for them! Dorothy, the CEO, is visible day and night when her team has terrific challenges, and we know she's humble because other CEOs, Glinda and the Wizard, respond well to her and want to work with her and because Toto leaps into her arms every chance he gets. Dogs know everything about people.

With leadership skills like these, not even a green-tinged, warty Witch and a seeming skyful of flying monkeys are able to prevail against Dorothy Gale's collaborative, collegial team. They work together to solve their challenges, using their emotional intelligence to make the most of their brain power—no more tornadoes of chaos and hysteria for them. Instead—integrity, courage, and empathy—ICE, the lucky bucket of water *frozen!*

It is not fair to ask others
what you are unwilling to do yourself.

ELEANOR ROOSEVELT

Chapter Six

———

POLAR BEARS

$\mathcal{I}$f integrity and courage are must-haves for good leadership, then where does the "E" fit into the formula? Before I go there, let me say once again that you absolutely must have integrity and courage to simply be a *good* leader. Those values are staples for good leadership. So if you know that you don't have them and you are placed into or assigned to a leadership role, here is my advice: get out of it! Don't do it, because if you are dishonest and cowardly, then you will be miserable in your role and so will the people you lead.

Once again, this is not theory. I have lived it. I have seen it happen time after time. In my years of management and leadership, I have seen everything—and this is no exaggeration, I mean *everything,* including physical and mental breakdowns—because people given the privilege of leadership lacked integrity and courage. So I say again, do yourself a big favor and do an even bigger favor for the people in your organization. If you have difficulty with the truth, or you have a hard time making courageous decisions, stop trying to lead. You can't do it. Resign yourself to being an individual contributor, not a leader of people.

The problem is that people who have a flawed value system usually do not recognize their own deficiencies. They often have a distorted view of themselves or they live in denial. As high-flying performers they may or may not realize their lack of ability to work with and care about other people, and they may not have a real desire to develop that ability. Either way, they have a blind spot, meaning they are sure to fail individually, and they are certain to fail the organization. By their lack of integrity and courage they create discontent in the organization.

The result is everything from dissension and retention problems, to disengagement and lack of production. Ultimately, the team spends more time at the water cooler discussing the leaders' character flaws than they do at their desks solving critical business issues. And all of that is costly to the organization and unfair to the people who depend upon you as a leader. That is why I am convinced that without integrity and courage, it is impossible to lead people.

Beyond integrity and courage, however, the next ingredient in the recipe is empathy. I believe it is truly the "secret sauce" that can take individuals to a special and rewarding level of leadership. Empathy—the "E" in ICE, along with integrity and courage—is what turns good leaders into great leaders. Listen to this: every great leader I have known or read about or worked for had well-defined empathy muscles. They had this wonderful ability to place themselves in other people's shoes and understand where they were coming from.

Before they made a statement or took some action, these leaders had the special ability to make their points and state their positions in a very caring way. Remember what my dad said many years ago? "People don't care how much you know until they know how much you care." That's empathy. If you truly follow his advice, it means you absolutely think about the people in your organization first! You consider everything they are experiencing before you act or speak. You realize that the person is easily as important as the business issue or situation at hand, if not more so.

This doesn't mean you are soft on performance. Actually, the contrary is more accurate. That is, the more empathetic you are with your people, the more performance you will get from them. Some of the best leaders I have worked with or for in my career were the most empathetic leaders. They were not pushover, touchy-feely types who were soft on performance. They were not just charismatic, flash-in-the-pan, ninety-day wonders, who show up one day with the next brilliant idea and then move on. They were consistent leaders who understood the importance of results, and they cherished the feelings of the people they led.

They took the time to demonstrate in a real way that they cared not only about the bottom line but also about those people who produced the results. The product of this honest and balanced empathetic style of leadership is not only that people enjoy where they work and stay there, but they also perform beyond expectations. The cold, hard fact is that people will go through brick walls for the leader who, in addition to integrity and courage and, of course, competence, displays empathy and an honest concern about the people he or she leads.

Okay, let's summarize. From my experience the best leaders are the steady leaders, the ones who understand the importance of results yet who cherish the feelings of the people they lead. Leading with empathy is a gentle balance, a middle ground between two opposite ends of the leadership spectrum—two polar opposites, the bleeding heart and the feared autocrat, and there are numerous iterations in between.

Extreme styles of leadership are destined to fail. They are single-dimensional, polar opposites, and each of them fails to mix appropriately the importance of the business issues with the importance of the people issues. Remarkably, corporations are full of people who are placed in positions of leadership but who operate close to these polar ends of the leadership spectrum. You'd think these leaders would be culled out before they reached positions of leadership, but so often these performers charm or bully their way to the top. It is unfortunate, but I have witnessed both extremes.

The bleeding heart may be loved by everyone because of an outgoing, caring nature, yet he or she proves to be ineffective when it comes to having a sound understanding of the business issues or being a person who can make tough decisions on time. They typically impress and endear themselves to you in the early days of their ascendancy through their warmth and openness, but very soon people realize that the business is suffering because this type of leader lacks business acumen and tends to focus on superficial issues.

These leaders may be the ones who remembers all the staff birthdays and anniversaries. They may be the first to offer support during a personal crisis, but they are also the ones who have difficulty navigating through a financial crisis or a delicate business case with a valued customer. And they really struggle with personnel decisions. They are content to leave ineffective people in their roles because they want more than anything to be viewed as good guys who make no waves.

Ultimately they fail, but not only do they fail themselves, they fail the organization and they fail the people they were obligated to lead. The result is low morale, distraction, and loss of competitive advantage. In competitive industries like pharmaceuticals, this type of weak leadership creates significant reorganizations and restructurings. Ironically, the bleeding heart, who has a soft spot for the people in his or her organization, subsequently builds a situation that comes back to haunt and hurt a lot of these same individuals—because many of them lose their jobs in a restructuring.

Additionally, the bleeding-heart leader typically makes decisions by building consensus. Whether this is a function of their lack of business confidence or their desire to please everyone in their group, the result is the same. The organization becomes paralyzed and frustrated. If the competition is perceptive, they can utilize this leadership void as an advantage in the marketplace. Your lost time and wheel-spinning become your competitor's golden opportunity to make up time and gain competitive traction. This style of leadership—weak on business issues and too empathetic about the people being led, results in a detrimental business environment. The spiral is ever downward, and the organization becomes severely compromised.

On the other hand, at the opposite end of this spectrum is the feared autocrat. This person is the polar opposite of the bleeding heart, a real "polar bear." The feared autocrat is the leader who rarely endears himself or herself to anyone, but who everybody respects because of their knowledge of the business. Typically, this person does not appear to have a caring bone in his or her body, but from a technical perspective, they are exceptional. They make clear and usually sound business decisions because they really do understand the business issues from soup to nuts. No one in their right mind would challenge this leader's business rationale.

This type of leader knows from experience or by intuition what needs to be done to get from point A to point B, even if that means gunning it down the highway and leaving lots of road kill along the way. This style of leader is so focused on the results that they are blind to the effect that this approach has on team individuals or the team's collective morale. Additionally, this style is stifling when it comes to development of those in positions below the autocrat's since he or she usually has his or her fingerprints all over each decision. Therefore, others don't get the practice they need to become competent, strong leaders themselves.

The feared autocrat is well versed in the strategy of the business. He or she truly understands the dynamics of the market. They can dissect a business case from every possible angle and they can evaluate performance issues in their sleep. They are skilled technicians. They are steely-eyed business surgeons who see the business issues, but they are blind to the feelings and emotions of the people they lead. And if they aren't blind, if they *do* understand what their people are feeling, they don't care, preferring instead to emphasize the ends of the strategy rather than the means to the goal or the amount of potential collateral damage.

Unfortunately, in terms of empathy this style of leadership, just like the bleeding heart, is also a recipe for disaster. The autocrat, in addition to expertise about the business, typically utilizes fear and intimidation as their primary tools to get results. Now there is no doubt that fear is an effective motivational tool. The only problem is that it is short lived, very short lived.

Humans are animals, so like any animal humans have a biological response to fear. That reaction regardless of the setting consists of one of two responses: either fight or flight. If you walk through a forest and come face to face with a bear, biologically your body will respond by releasing adrenaline. Your brain will then signal you either to fight the bear or to flee from it. There is nothing in between.

The same thing occurs much more subtly in the business world. If your boss is an autocratic leader, one who leads through fear and intimidation, you face the corporate bear in the corporate forest every day. Of course, your physical life is not in immediate danger, but in due time you will realize that your career, your business life, is threatened. It is threatened by a person in charge who is so focused on results that they scare the living daylights out of you.

Each night you go home either perplexed about what is happening to you or frightened that you may make an honest mistake that will have a significant and detrimental effect on your career. Although you may not realize it, over time your business adrenaline will start to build, and your brain will signal you to select between two career options, fight or flight. It is simply human nature. When we are faced with fear and intimidation, we either face it or we run away.

This is exactly what happens to individuals who work for the feared, autocratic leader. At first, the team digs in and tries as hard as they can to please the boss. After a period of time, however, they get so beaten down or so intimidated that they either work against the boss ("fight the polar bear") or they opt to work somewhere else ("flight from the polar bear"). Either way, the result once again is bad for everyone and costly to the organization.

Back in the late 1980s and early 1990s as we were building the managed care department, I worked directly for a really good guy, Bill Baicy. Bill was a very astute businessman and a person of absolute, uncompromising integrity. Like me, he was a long-timer with Glaxo, having started there in the late seventies. When we launched Zantac, Bill was the entire market research department for the company.

His responsibility was to run the predictive models and figure out how many dollars of each product we would sell in a given year versus how much we needed to invest in sales force and marketing expenditures to drive those dollars. Since Bill's job involved adding up the numbers and since his last name was Baicy, we just referred to him as "The Count."

Bill suggested to me that it might be a good idea to bring the managed care group together for some strategic planning and much-needed team building since the group had grown to twelve people. He further suggested that I hire an outside consulting firm, the Center for Creative Leadership (CCL), out of Greensboro, North Carolina, to facilitate the meeting. I followed Bill's advice and set up a three-day offsite meeting. The first day was dedicated to team building, and the following two days were for strategy.

The Center for Creative Leadership sent a facilitator named Stan to run our first day's training. All twelve people from the managed care department were there, including two of my direct reports: Chris Carney, who headed up managed care marketing programs, and Clint Burrus, who ran the managed care field force. Additionally, my boss, Count Baicy, was in attendance.

The program began as most of these do, with introductions, followed by the customary ice-breaker. Stan instructed each of us to state our birth date and then to share with the group something about ourselves that no one else knew. (By the way, there is almost a 100 percent probability that if more than fifty people are assembled in a room, at least two of them will have the same birthday. Try it the next time you have a large group of people together!)

The agenda for Day One was simple. Stan would provide some didactic presentations in the first part of the morning about team dynamics and give examples of effective teams. This would be followed by two group exercises designed to diagnose and evaluate our team behaviors, and then we would close the day with a debriefing or postmortem of lessons learned.

After Stan's presentations we were ready to go. He handed out the first exercise. The situation and instructions were as follows:

> Your team is on the way to a skiing week in a very secluded place when your van breaks down. The temperature is below zero degrees Fahrenheit and you are in the midst of a blizzard. You have only three

tools—a knife, a car jack, and a lighter. Your mission
is to formulate a survival plan that will work until
help arrives.

We broke out to develop our plan for survival. When we
returned to the meeting room, we all high-fived each other, then
we shared our plan. Stan listened closely, then informed us that
two things about our work stood out. One was that our plan would
result in virtually no chance of survival for anyone in the group.
We would have frozen to death before anyone would be able to
save us. The other and more important observation was that we
had made our decisions as a team—with unity, commitment, and
solidarity. "It was an impressive team effort," he told us.

We broke for lunch, and I was feeling really good about how
well the team had worked together on our previous exercise,
notwithstanding the fact that by the time the rescue team arrived
we would have been twelve human icicles huddled in or near the
broken-down vehicle.

After lunch Stan handed out our second team-building
exercise. Once again, the instructions were very simple. Our
moderator divided the team into two groups: the Strategists, to
which my field leader, Clint Burrus, and I were assigned; and the
Implementers, to which Chris Carney and several of our account
managers were assigned. Each team was secluded in its own room
with a separate set of directions, but neither team was privy to the
other's instructions. We were told to complete the exercise and
reconvene in half an hour.

My group's instructions were as follows:

> The Implementers will be given several geometric
> puzzle pieces, such as triangles, squares, rectangles,
> trapezoids, and rhombuses. When assembled cor-
> rectly, they will form a perfect square. As Strategists
> you are to figure out the correct alignment of the
> puzzle pieces, and then you are to instruct the Imple-
> menters on how to build the square. The only stipu-
> lation is that you cannot use any verbal direction.

The Implementers' instructions were almost identical, except
that they were told that they could not ask for any verbal direction.
The instructions were to be driven primarily by the Strategists.
The Implementers could, however, make their own suggestions on
how to complete the exercise, both verbally and nonverbally.

Once I read our instructions to our team, the Strategists, I
immediately concluded that the contest must be one of time to
completion, instead of one of team cooperation. I decided we
needed to take the bull by the horns and develop a very simple
communications plan for the Implementers that required no
thinking on their part and no input from anyone, especially themselves. Remember, to me time was of the essence and I had no
interest in anything that was going to cause a delay. And it didn't
help that Stan was standing there with a stopwatch in his hand.

Once the Implementers returned to the meeting room, I
isolated one of the members of their group and sat him down at a

table upon which we had drawn the face of a clock. I handed him the geometric puzzle pieces that we had numbered 1 through 12. It took him about ten seconds to build the square! By the time I looked up, ready to bask in the glory of some new record for time to completion, I noticed that everyone looked disappointed, if not disgusted. I remember thinking, *What's wrong? We did it in record time.*

When Chris Carney and Clint Burrus finally spoke up, they told me emphatically that my behavior in completing this exercise was exactly how I had been managing in general. They gave pretty convincing examples of situations in which I would micromanage everything at work and not provide them with opportunities for input or suggestions. They were being totally honest, I could see; there was nothing at all manipulative about what they were doing and saying.

Finally Chris, who in addition to being a co-worker is one of my best friends, said something that will stick with me forever: "Steve, if you are going to continue like this, I don't want to work for you anymore." Wow! You talk about a splash of cold water in the face! I had no idea that my competitive drive and results-orientation had driven me so far toward operating like such an autocrat, a corporate bear.

In less than eight hours, I had witnessed two vivid examples of a team in action, one at its best and one at its worst. The only difference between the two examples was that in the second, my behavior as an autocratic leader was eroding the foundation of a truly cohesive unit. It took the courage and honesty of Clint and Chris right there in front of my boss, the department, and the facilitator to help me realize that I don't always have the answers and that involvement of the team is just as important as how fast I reach the result.

To think that my two direct reports and trusted friends were so frustrated with me that they considered leaving the group provided me with a much-needed slice of humble pie. I wonder how many times those members of the managed care team had had a sidebar conversation or a water-cooler discussion in which they talked about how frustrated they were or, worse yet, talked about leaving the organization.

Make no mistake about it, yours truly was behaving as a corporate bear. Through the honesty of two of my trusted friends and colleagues, I learned a valuable lesson and that is — you catch more bears with honey than you do with vinegar.

Never tell people how to do things.
Tell them what to do, and they will
surprise you with their ingenuity.

GENERAL GEORGE PATTON

Chapter Seven

———

SWEET SPOT

$\mathcal{N}$ow that we have established the two polar ends of the leadership spectrum, it's a lot of fun to use that knowledge to look around us in the workplace and be a critic. It's easy to see these extremes everywhere! And it's easy to point the finger of blame at others. The difficult question to answer for our own personal development, though, is where is the sweet spot of leadership—the perfect place between the two polar ends from which to lead?

In the science of baseball, the sweet spot is the center of percussion. They call it the fat of the bat, and it is the best place to hit the ball if the batter wants to hear a solid, gut-satisfying sound and get a good result. The same is true in racquetball, tennis, and golf—learning to hit the ball on the sweet spot of the racquet or

club will bring a better game to the player who practices, practices, and practices some more.

The same is true in the corporate game. The leader who,
in addition to demonstrating integrity and courage, is able to
balance the hard skills (the business competencies) with the
soft skills (the emotions) has found the sweet spot of leadership.
Empathetic leaders, as the name implies, *do* care, but they also *do*
lead. They can and do make tough business decisions, including
difficult personnel decisions, because they truly understand the
business and they realize that what needs to be done to move
their organizations forward is often consistent with the best
interests of the people in the organization.

These leaders are usually quite experienced and well grounded
in the business fundamentals of their company and their industry.
Empathetic leaders also have an acute awareness of the feelings of
the people they lead. Like my dad was, they, too, are visible to the
people in the organization, and they are almost always approachable individuals. People at all levels of their organization have
little difficulty interacting with this type of leader. I like to think
of this leader as the model of the benevolent dictator. He or she
has learned to lead from the sweet spot.

"Dictator" may sound too strong a characterization because it
conjures up images of Adolf Hitler, Benito Mussolini, or Saddam
Hussein. The hard truth, however, about dictators is that they
almost always have a vision. They are decisive, and they certainly
understand the strategies and tactics that need to be employed
to move people to carry out their vision. In the examples mentioned above, there is no doubt that stubbornness, ruthlessness,

and complete disregard for enemies were major weaknesses that resulted in the demise of these three dictators, and ultimately in the demise of the people who followed them.

Leaving that aside for a minute, however, and focusing on the positives, leaders in business must never be afraid to be dictatorial. When it comes to defining direction, creating strategy, and making tough decisions, people want to feel that their leader has a vision for the organization, understands the external marketplace, and can resolve important conflicts to their benefit. All of these are the strengths of dictators.

Organizational psychologists like my friend Karol might say that these competencies have to do with left-brain function, which includes logic, analysis, and linear thought processes. Emphasizing left-brain function makes dictatorial competencies single-dimensional, having little to do with what the team desires and fears the most. But wait! The great leader also has effective right-brain function, including the abilities to conceptualize, to relate to people, and to think laterally. Therefore, the complete leader, in my estimation and experience, is the benevolent (right brain) dictator (left brain).

Here is where empathy plays a key role. For those leaders who have the competencies and the hard skills, empathy enables them to function effectively by employing total-brain leadership. They then operate in a balanced manner, one where they drive for results yet are considerate of the emotions and problems of the people they lead. Benevolent dictators are secure enough to share their ideas with their people, but they also listen to and consider in return the ideas their people have. They have a good sense of where to go and what to do, but because of their right-brain function they seek and encourage input from their teams. As a result of this intellectual give-and-take, their decisions are better informed and their teams are more committed.

Most important, the benevolent dictator really cares about the people he or she leads. This type of leader is tuned in to his or her people, and the benevolent dictator takes the time to say things and do things that reinforce in a genuine way just how much they care. They are unafraid to let their emotional guard down, to wear their hearts on their sleeves, and to allow people to see them in candid, human ways.

Early in my career, I was mentored at Glaxo by someone who had a significant impact on me. He was, in my opinion, the classic benevolent dictator. He had that balanced mix of right- and left-brain function, and like my dad, he had an important impact on my life, as well as on my own approach to leadership. His name was Jim Butler. Even today before I take an action in a critical situation, whether it is a business issue or a personal issue, I often think to myself, *How would Jim handle this?* Many of the people who have worked with me can attest to the fact that I often say, "Jim would do it this way" or "Jim would do it that way."

Jim led from the sweet spot, and I'm working to follow him in that type of leadership. It's not that I don't understand the business or don't have my own finger on the emotional pulse of my organization. It is that, like the Carly Simon song says, "Nobody does it better" than Jim Butler did, and I was fortunate to learn from his example and from his mentoring.

When I joined Glaxo in November 1980, I met Jim at my

initial sales training class in Fort Lauderdale, Florida. At that time, Jim was Glaxo's national sales manager. We were informed by our sales trainer that periodically during the program Jim would stop by to say hello and to check on our progress, then join us for dinner on the last evening of the week we were in training. I was impressed by this. The head guy, our company's national sales manager, was going to spend some significant time with a group of about fifteen new salespeople! In my mind's eye, I pictured him to be quite different than he would turn out to be.

Let me put this in perspective to give you a sense of how small Glaxo was back then. Our entire training program consisted of one week at the home office in Florida and a little bit of home study. As I mentioned before, we only had two product lines, our Vicon line, an assortment of vitamins, and a prescription medicine called Corticaine Cream, our "flagship" rectal medicine. Our annual sales total in the United States was $6 million. This lack of sophistica-tion of our medicines did not require a lot of scientific training.

Today the story is quite different. We have so many compli-cated medicines that make up our $20-plus-billion company that it takes a training department almost as big as *all* of Glaxo back in 1980 to do the job. Instead of one week, the initial training program today is about six months long.

That being said, in Fort Lauderdale at my initial sales training class, Jim Butler was a frequent visitor to the class. He was billed to us as "the salespersons' sales manager," so I expected to see this booming, charming, charismatic, corporate-looking guy right out of some Zig Ziglar sales program. Nothing could have been further from the truth. He looked nothing like the person I was expecting to see. Instead, Jim was and still is a low-key individual, unassuming, private, and quiet.

Actually, my first impression of Jim was that he was not overly warm or, for that matter, overly friendly. He came across physically as quiet and very serious, like Don Corleone in *The Godfather*. He had an intimidating look in his eyes, a light complexion, light-colored hair, and he always dressed immaculately. As promised, he spent a lot of time with us that week, yet he said very little. In fact, I found it difficult to have a conversation with this man, and during the first four years when I was a sales representative, even after I got to know him a lot better, I still found Jim somewhat difficult to talk with.

From 1981 to 1984, we had a number of major new product launches. We had Ventolin for asthma, Beconase for allergies, Zinacef for bacterial infections, Zantac for ulcers, and Trandate for high blood pressure. For each of these launches we came together for a national sales meeting. Jim was always present, but my perception of him at these events was not that much different than it had been at my initial sales training class.

This man was just a tough guy to talk to, and believe me, I tried hard to engage him in conversation! I tried to talk with him about sports. About the business. About family. Although he was always very cordial and his affect was never anything less than respectful, his conventional style, to be honest, was very reserved. Jim usually gave me one-word answers, simple sentences, or perhaps a polite nod of the head. On the surface there wasn't a lot of effervescence or, for that matter, much exuberance. Little did I know....

The perplexing and interesting thing for me was that every

time he was introduced at our sales meetings, he would get a great response. Most times it was a standing ovation, and the salespeople who had been around the longest, the ones who knew him the best, were the ones who responded the loudest. They just loved the guy. Just goes to show that you should never judge a book by its cover.

So I thought, *What is it about Jim Butler that causes so many people to react with so much honest respect and affection? Is it his competence?* There is no doubt that Jim knew then and today still knows the key issues on the commercial side of the pharmaceutical business. He is an extremely wise and talented person when it comes to knowledge of the pharmaceutical marketplace and how to build effective strategies.

In the early 1980s, under Jim's stewardship, the Glaxo sales force became the envy of the pharmaceutical industry. We were launching new product after new product. Under his direction we were investing heavily in the commercial success of our medicines and were exceeding everyone's sales expectations. Our asthma medicine, Ventolin, became the number-one inhaled prescription medicine for asthma after one year on the market. Zantac, our blockbuster, quickly surpassed SmithKline's Tagamet in market share in just two and a half years to become the most successful product ever launched in the United States. And our injectable antibiotics, Zinacef and Fortaz, were quickly gaining significant traction in the hospital market, which had been dominated by the pharmaceutical giant Eli Lilly. All of this occurred under Jim Butler's leadership. These medicines were surely important advances, but it was Jim's knowledge of the market that made them so successful. All of us, including the employees and our shareholders, benefited from his business savvy as Glaxo's stock quadrupled during this period.

Here's another example of his knowledge of our business. In 1986, Jim came to me and asked me to take on the task of heading up Glaxo's managed care efforts. He had the perception that third-party payers, such as HMOs, insurance companies, and our state and federal governments, were going to have a big impact on our business. He believed back then that these types of organizations would build systems and processes that would either enhance or preclude patient access to our medicines. This was at a time when most pharmaceutical executives could not even spell HMO. Today, nearly 90 percent of GlaxoSmithKline's $20 billion of sales is made by means of contracts with one of these organizations. Back in 1986, that figure was less than 10 percent. How insightful Jim was!

When I accepted the position of Manager of Managed Care, Jim told me something that has stuck with me for a long time— the same advice I share with people in our organization today. He told me, "Make sure you get out and ask your customers to teach you about their business, because then they will become like any other teacher. They will have a vested interest in your success." He was absolutely correct. That advice was a stroke of genius, and I followed it to the letter.

His advice was simple enough, but also profound. By following what Jim had said, it didn't take us long at all to position Glaxo strongly in the managed care market. We started addressing managed care in a formalized and structured way in 1986, and within one year we had leapfrogged the rest of our industry when we were ranked first in every third-party survey as the most effective pharmaceutical company addressing the managed care marketplace. Measuring the number of contacts and the quality of those contacts, we were clearly the industry leader. Jim's insight into the changing dynamics of our business as well as his advice to me to let our customers teach me about their business enabled us to position Glaxo well in the managed care market.

Jim's perception of where the business was going was, as the British say, spot-on, and his advice about how to learn the market was also correct. He had dictator qualities in that he knew the direction that we must go. He had unwavering vision. Also, he understood the strategies and tactics we needed to employ, and he was decisive—*very* decisive.

His timing and instincts could not have been more precise. As a result, Glaxo was hitting home run after home run. In December 1986, I attended my first Managed Care Customer Meeting. Back then it was called the HMO Pharmacy Directors' Symposium and was held at the MGM Grand in Las Vegas. I met Bob Navarro and Hank Blissenbach there—two pharmacy directors from a powerful HMO headquartered in Minnesota, Physician's Health Plan. Their corporate headquarters was located in Minneapolis, but they also managed plans in other regions of the country, like New England and the Mid-Atlantic. Ultimately this HMO became United Healthcare, which as of this writing is one of the country's largest, most profitable, and most influential managed care companies. Additionally, Physician's Health Plan created a pharmacy benefit company named Diversified Pharmacy Services, which they sold to SmithKline in 1994 for almost $3 billion.

When I first met Bob and Hank at the MGM Grand, I expected the usual drink, small talk, and patronizing discussion about how we could work together. Instead, I got an intense lecture about how they were looking very seriously at the anti-ulcer therapeutic category, and how they were going to select only one histamine-two (H$_2$) antagonist for their formulary. In their own words, while we sipped on our cocktails, it was either going to be Tagamet from SmithKline or Zantac from Glaxo.

Wow, you talk about baptism by fire! I had been in the job for less than two months. I was following Jim's advice to let my customers teach me, but now I was faced with a very serious challenge. In my heart, I believed that Zantac was a better medicine than Tagamet. But I also knew that these guys weren't totally buying into our value proposition.

They had determined that Zantac offered clinical benefits over Tagamet, but they were not sure that Zantac was worth the 20 percent price premium that it commanded. In addition, the anti-ulcer category was easily their most costly category from a pharmaceutical perspective. So their strategy was to leverage their size and strength and get either Glaxo or SmithKline to break on price.

For both Glaxo and SmithKline this was a serious situation. For Glaxo, however, this was a *critical* situation. Although we were introducing a lot of new medicines during the 1980s, more than 80 percent of our sales revenue accrued to one product, Zantac. We also believed that if this managed care plan could restrict access to Zantac, then other HMOs would follow in their footsteps. We believed other managed care companies would sit back, watch, and evaluate PHP's actions and develop similar strategies in this therapeutic category. Our major concern was that one by one large insurers and HMOs would come to us requesting bids and price concessions on our company's critical medicine—Zantac.

When I returned from Vegas, I went directly to Jim to get his advice on how to deal with this challenge. The first thing he did was calm me down. He said something like, "Everything's going to be okay, Steve. Just develop a contracting strategy that ensures that we maintain the Zantac franchise at PHP without being transparent to our competition." That was it. No other words of wisdom, no definitive suggestions on how to structure the deal. He wanted me to figure it out, and he wanted me to become the person who built an effective contracting strategy.

That advice, however, was just the start of his leadership and support on this challenge. For the next nine months, from January through September of 1987, we met often to negotiate with the decision makers at PHP; each time we met with them, Jim was there right next to me providing support, encouragement, and direction. When push came to shove, there was no way he would be a headquarters general. Jim's preference was to be in the trenches on the front lines, eyeball to eyeball with the customer, making sure they knew our position and making sure they knew we would deliver on our contractual obligations.

These months were a 90-degree learning curve for me. By the end of that period I had witnessed close up the fact that Jim Butler had the key leadership traits cited as far back as the seventeenth century by English scholar Franciscus Junius: "the heart to conceive, the understanding to direct, [and] the hand to execute." Like Jim's people, I, too, was in awe of the man.

Ultimately, we won the PHP contract. They selected Zantac as their only anti-ulcer (histamine-two antagonist) product. This was a huge win for us. It enabled us to position Zantac as the drug of choice for the treatment of ulcers in arguably one of the most aggressive managed care plans in the country. Clearly, other plans would notice that decision—and they did!

But back to the reaction that people had to Jim as a leader— why people would go through brick walls for him. It wasn't just his business acumen that was responsible for that kind of reaction. A number of senior people at Glaxo in the 1980s were visionary, smart, and experienced executives. We had folks like Alan Steigrod, vice president of sales and marketing; Joe Ruvane, president of Glaxo Inc.; Rich Franco, vice president of marketing; and Peter Wise, vice president of medical, just to name a few.

They were extremely competent and well-respected leaders in their fields. Their people and their teams certainly were respected, but it wasn't the same as with Jim Butler. There was something about the way Jim interacted with his people that forged a deeper relationship with him, and thus a deeper commitment to Glaxo. Although I was perplexed with the response to Jim in my very early days with Glaxo, it only took one experience for me to figure out why his people loved and admired him so much.

As I mentioned before, I was promoted to the home office as an associate training manager in 1984. My wife, Denise; our newborn, Jackie; and I left the comforts of home in Philly to start a new life. It was a huge challenge. Neither Denise nor I had ever lived far from home before we relocated to Raleigh, North Carolina. In addition to having a new child, we now had a new house, and I had a new career. There was a ton of change in our lives, and all of it was coming at us at the same time.

By January 1985, we had moved into our brand-new house, and I was preparing to train my first class of approximately forty sales representatives. On the Sunday evening before the class began, I completed all my preparation and went to bed. Our sales reps were housed at the North Raleigh Hilton about three miles from our house.

At this time, Glaxo was not yet a profitable subsidiary in the United States, so we did not have enough money to build or own a training facility. All of our training was done offsite in hotels. Today we have a state-of-the-art training facility about sixty thousand square feet in size on our campus in Research Triangle Park, North Carolina.

As a young, up-and-coming professional getting ready to train my first sales class, I was full of energy, ambition, and enthusiasm. And let me be honest, at this time I was also full of myself! I knew this was a chance to show my goods and ultimately move up the corporate ladder. Nothing was going to get in my way.

During that Sunday night, however, there was a big-time ice storm in the Raleigh area that resulted in loss of electricity and heat to many homes, including ours. When I awoke on Monday morning to a cold, dark house, I was faced with a decision. I could either leave my wife and infant daughter to fend for themselves or I could stay home and miss the opening day of our new sales class.

Missing the class would have been okay. Glaxo, like almost

every other business in the area, was closed that day. In North Carolina when there is an ice or snow storm, everything shuts down. We depend on one snow-removal company—"God's Snow Removal," the sun! But I knew the class was already housed in the hotel only three miles away. So I made what I thought was a noble and empathetic decision. I lit the fireplace, made sure Denise and Jackie were wrapped snugly in warm clothes and blankets, and went off to the class. I rationalized that I had a job to do and nothing was going to get in my way.

So on Monday morning I was up in front of the sales class teaching my heart out when I saw the door at the back of the room open. In walked the man himself—our head of sales, Mr. Butler. He motioned me to the back of the room. I excused myself from the class, and as I walked toward Jim, I remember smiling, expecting a pat on the back for braving the elements to get to the training program. Instead, he gave me a polite kick in the pants for leaving my wife and daughter alone without heat or electricity. Then he told me something that has stuck with me and will stick with me forever: "Steve, this morning I drove to your house and picked up Denise and Jackie. I took them to our house where I want them to stay until things are back to normal again. We'll look after them—with Denise new to the area, she's probably not used to this kind of emergency, is she? You come on over when you're through here."

This was our head of sales—the top guy! He was way up there on the corporate ladder, yet he was looking out for someone way down there like me, an associate manager. At that moment I figured out why Jim's people appreciated him so much and why he was such an admired leader.

When I completed the day's training session, as instructed I too went to Jim's house. When I arrived I found that in addition to my family, Jim had rounded up some other families, like the Coughlins—Bobby, Margie, Timmy, and Kelly. Bobby also worked for him and they were in the same predicament. They, too, would stay at Jim's house until their situation got back to normal.

I worked either directly or indirectly for Jim for ten years. He was smart, strategic, and tough as nails when it came to the business. His secret, though, the reason people would run the extra mile for him, was that in addition to his core business skills, he had empathy. He honestly cared for his people, and he was unafraid to show it. Whether you call it emotional intelligence, total-brain leadership, or the benevolent dictator model, Jim led by staying in the sweet spot.

He modeled organizational stewardship better than anyone I ever worked for because he demonstrated integrity and courage and because he had that perfect balance of justice and mercy in his character—empathy. He wasn't a bleeding heart, and, on the other hand, he wasn't a tyrant. From his response to that icy day in 1985, there was no doubt in my mind that Jim Butler was a special leader. He practiced what my dad told me: "Always, always remember that people don't care how much you know until they know how much you care."

In 1993, Jim left Glaxo, and I assumed a lot of his responsibilities. Jim was ready to move on and do some different things, and Glaxo was going through a period of change, with a lot of new senior talent coming into the organization from other companies. On the night he finally decided to move on, Jim and his wife,

Sheila, took Denise and me to dinner at his favorite restaurant, Nick's. Today it is called Jimmy V's, after the late basketball coach at North Carolina State University, Jim Valvano. As you might expect, Jim Butler knew everyone in the place, including the owner, the bartender, and the waitresses.

Once we were seated, Jim ordered a couple of bottles of Dom Perignon and then asked all the staff to gather around our table. He poured each one a glass of champagne. He then told everyone about his decision to leave Glaxo and my promotion to his position. He told everyone that I would be the new boss, and then he made a toast to me and to my family's success. Once the toast was finished and we all clicked glasses for luck, I leaned toward him and whispered that I was a little bit uncomfortable since I was assuming a lot of his role.

Jim Butler, the salesperson's sales manager and classic benevolent dictator, looked at me with those piercing eyes for a moment—a total-brain look if I've ever seen one! Then with a little smile he said, "That's why you train people and later turn the job over to them—so that you can see the people you love grow and succeed. Now it's *your* turn." My turn—to practice leadership to the best of my ability every day, behaving with integrity and courage. But also my turn to practice leading from the sweet spot of empathy—the perfect place on the bat that sends the business forward and clears the bases for four runners to come on home—to cheers, applause, and perhaps to a standing ovation like the ones they gave to Jim Butler.

I am not one of those who believe
a great army is the means of maintaining peace,
because if you build up a great profession those who
form parts of it want to exercise their profession.

Woodrow Wilson

Chapter Eight

———

GO TO THE GYM

$\mathcal{B}$y now I expect there's no doubt in your mind that I am totally committed to the importance of having and demonstrating leadership values. Solid leadership values like integrity, courage, and empathy are an integral part of the foundation of high-quality leadership. Without them, I believe it is impossible for me or anyone, for that matter, to be an effective leader. So I make a conscious effort not only to incorporate them into the fabric of my team, but also to apply these values as Tiger Woods does—by seeking and measuring them for continual improvement. And I mean a real and personal commitment to how well I develop and fine-tune them.

It's like developing physical fitness. As an avid jogger and fitness freak, I know that if I get lazy and regularly miss my workouts, the results will show up in the mirror. I will see, unless I am in denial, weight gain, loss of muscle tone, and fatigue. So I take the same approach to developing leadership values. I think about integrity, courage, and empathy as leadership muscles; just as with building up and maintaining strong biceps, triceps, and trapezoids, I need to go to the "values gym" and work them out on a routine schedule so that these "muscles" do not lose their tone and so that I don't get flabby and lazy in my approach to leading people. Complacency will ruin your business as thoroughly as dishonesty.

In the case of leadership muscles, however, the routine is so much more convenient. There's no gym to join, and no jogging shoes or exercise clothes to remember. Everything is right there in front of you at your place of employment. All you need to do is to make the connection between your normal workplace activities and the special opportunities to exercise your leadership muscles.

Strategy sessions, group presentations, employee reviews, customer meetings, and new-product launches are perfect activities for a good workout! Just consider for a moment the number of times you interact with people in your organization in these types of settings. Every occasion of this type is like a piece of exercise equipment in a gym that provides you with the chance to flex those ICE muscles until they burn from fatigue and exhaustion. By the end of the day you become a firmer, fitter, and better corporate athlete.

All you need to do is make a connection, thinking consciously about how you make every decision or state each statement with awareness about its integrity, courage, and empathy. Does each decision and statement measure up? If not, then tomorrow you can work harder to decrease the discrepancy between what you observe yourself doing or saying and what you intend to do or say.

That's working your ICE muscles. It's no different from making a conscious decision to do three sets of fifteen repetitions on the bicep, tricep, and trapezoid machines when you are in the gym. The results are the same. You improve. You look better. You feel better about your work and your career, and you create more value for your organization.

Now I mentioned a few obvious areas where you get to exercise the ICE muscles—strategy sessions, group presentations, new-product launches, customer meetings, and, most important, performance reviews. Before I get to performance reviews, however, let me ask you a question. Take a few seconds to think about it. Here goes: If you are leading a sales and marketing team, how much more would you sell if your customers viewed your team as honest and courageous as well as truly empathetic to their needs? Now take that question one step further. If you are leading a sales and marketing team, how much more would your team *want* to sell if they viewed *you* as an honest, courageous, and caring leader? These questions are rhetorical and, of course, their answers are obvious. It's as obvious as asking how much better would you look and feel if you ran twenty miles every week and lifted weights three times a week.

One thing that really irritates me, though, is when people assume that leaders are born, not made. This assumption is flat-out wrong from a number of perspectives, but I will highlight just two of them. First, it doesn't give good leaders credit for their self-awareness, conviction, and discipline in exercising and building their leadership skills. These individuals are very much in tune with their effect, both positive and negative, on the people they lead. They want to make sure that their impact enhances the team's ability to meet its mission through consistent and appropriate behavior. They are the ones who seek honest and constructive feedback. They are the ones who have learned that in almost all situations the process is just as important as the product, and they use successful outcomes in process to measure leadership improvement.

Second, the misconception that leaders are born not made allows for a nice excuse for lazy leaders to escape accountability for their poor leadership skills. These corporate pythons get a pass on leadership values because people's expectations are to accept their penchant for production and not hold them responsible for modeling leadership behavior. For them the results are all that matter; they have little regard for the process or the people along the way. They do not practice organizational stewardship because it is all about the bottom line. For them, employee roadkill, the bodies left strewn along their paths, are nothing more than collateral damage, simply an occupational hazard. Over time, just like a python, they suffocate the life out of any organization. Yet they get a pass for a while, and they get that pass because they are viewed as competent through a single trait, their productivity. They get it because people believe leadership values are like eye color or physical stature—a function of DNA, not hard work.

But nothing is further from the truth. Leadership values can and should be learned from the time we are children until the time we slip on our gold watches and hang up our corporate cleats. As children, it starts with the people around us—our parents, siblings, teachers, and friends. These people initially set our leadership compass in the right direction. During these early years, we are by nature sponges. From an educational perspective, we are at our most fertile time to learn. That's why childhood is referred to as our formative years—our beliefs, intellect, and emotions take form. We learn reading, writing, arithmetic, languages, athletics, music, art, and, yes, values. As children, we need to be taught at a very early age the difference between right and wrong because we just soak it up in those years.

I was fortunate in this regard. I lived with my parents and grandparents as well as my brother. Not much was special about my childhood. It was as normal as could be. It was, however, exceptional when it came to values. Everyone in our house as well as most of my extended family—aunts, uncles, and cousins—believed and practiced good values. So early on, growing up in a blue-collar town outside of Philadelphia, I had many good role models who demonstrated and practiced solid values, like being honest and caring for each other. I could see that life worked to everyone's benefit if we valued and practiced integrity, courage, and empathy.

But it doesn't end there. Once we get beyond our formative years, once we finish our formal education and become gainfully employed in the workplace, learning about leadership gets a turbo charge. Just as with our families, we see people in significant role-model positions during our formative years in the corporation, and their leadership styles can make a lasting imprint on our own behaviors. If they are effective leaders—are productive and demonstrate good leadership skills—we should emulate what they do. From the start, we should lean on them heavily as mentors, so that they can pass on to us the gems that have enabled them to be such successful leaders in their careers. Think about that first real boss or that first corporate executive where one's inner self made the connection and told you, "I want to be like him/her."

For me, that happened in 1981. Glaxo was launching our new medicine for asthma, Ventolin, and it was my first experience at a national launch meeting. About two hundred of us, mostly salespeople, were in attendance at the Marriott Hotel in Fort Lauderdale, Florida. We arrived on a Sunday afternoon, and that evening we had our reception dinner. At the head table were all our dignitaries, our president Charley Hart and his direct reports, maybe nine or ten people. Charley Hart handled the usual corporate introductions. There was semi-polite attention, then perfunctory applause, followed by the usual chatter among the salespeople—that is, until Charley introduced our head of sales, Jim Butler. First there was complete silence, and once he finished introducing Jim, a standing ovation and thundering applause seemed to last forever. At that exact moment I remember being puzzled, thinking, *Wow, that was different! How wonderful it must be for someone to get that much respect and admiration.* I wanted to find out what it took to get into a position where I would have that effect on the people I led.

This reminds me of something Malcolm S. Forbes wrote in 1980, right about the time of my first product launch meeting:

> Silence is the ultimate applause. *Newsweek* had a piece a while ago about Vladimir Horowitz, "the world's greatest pianist." It ends with Ed Behr, regional editor, asking Horowitz if he "still gets a kick

out of applause." Replies the maestro, "It's the silence that matters, not the applause. Anyone can have applause. But the silence, before and during the playing—that is everything." Isn't that an absolute truth? For artists, particularly performing ones, rapt attention is reflected by total silence. Rustling, shuffling, whispers all signal an audience unentranced. (*Forbes*, August 13, 2007, p. 120)

Once again, fortune shone on me, as, except for my father, Jim became the most important influence on my professional career, and it did not take long for him to become my mentor. Mentoring is critical in building our leadership muscles. Think of mentors as personal trainers who work with us day in and day out to continue to challenge us to build our leadership strength. Jim wasn't just any mentor, he was ideal for the role because he was the guy I wanted to be, not just because of his success but because I recognized that people respected how he operated. So it wasn't only *what* Jim accomplished that I admired, but *how* he did it—the process.

I have been blessed many times in my career by mentors who have had a huge impact on my professional life. People like Bob Ingram, George Morrow, Sandy Costa, Tim Tyson, Chris Viehbacher, Mike Corrigan, and George Abercrombie—all senior executives at one time or another with Glaxo, GlaxoWellcome, GlaxoSmithKline, or whatever our name is when this book gets published, have had a significant impact on my leadership style, as well as on my approach to our business. I have learned something new and different from each of them, and in their own way each of these individuals has reinforced my own core beliefs in what good leadership is all about.

Thus, the art of leadership and specifically the application of leadership values are not simply functions of a biological process. They are not encoded into anyone's managerial DNA. The ability to practice good leadership is a listening and learning process. It doesn't occur unless we have opportunities to lead, mentors to help us grow, and a willingness to change so that we can improve. The willingness to change means that we *want to* work out our ICE muscles every chance we get to do so in the workplace, we *will practice* when we still fall short of the highest ICE values, and we *will measure* increments of improvement.

Biologically, two abilities that distinguish human beings from other animals on this planet are that humans have both the intellect to process sophisticated information and the free will to make informed and conscious decisions. These abilities provide the wiring for how we choose to behave, as well as the values we model. If you take it one step further, one layer deeper, our intellect and our free will govern how we interact with other human beings and how we live our daily existence.

Our intellect and free will allow us to make trade-offs and conscious decisions for which we should be held accountable and responsible. We decide whether to do things the right way or to compromise and rationalize our bad behaviors. We decide whether we are going to invest our time productively and improve or be complacent and let opportunities pass us by. We decide whether we are going to stay active and physically fit or become sedentary and out of shape. And, yes, we decide as leaders whether we are going to work to become very productive leaders who seek opportunities to build our leadership skills and those of our teams.

So how do you do it? Imagine this setting. You are leading an organization of twenty thousand people. Ultimately your responsibility is to set the direction, endorse the strategy, empower the organization, as well as to align rewards with successful performance and appropriate behaviors. This is the ideal setting to work out your ICE muscles. It is the Gold's Gym or L.A. Fitness Center for building leadership values.

First, you model leadership behavior every chance you get. Individuals on sports teams or on any team follow what the leader does and how the leader acts. If you truly believe the concept that the process is as important as the product, and you are fully committed to fostering appropriate behaviors in the organization, then here is a simple plan to consider:

1. Define the mission and the vision for the organization.
2. Set measurable goals and objectives that are aligned with the mission and the vision.
3. Identify behaviors and values by which you want your team to operate. Communicate them clearly and often, but don't preach; use stories, examples, facts, statistics, analogies, and other comparisons as means of illustrating or showing them the values you want.
4. Institute a rewards and recognition program consistent with the goals, objectives, and behaviors you want your team to demonstrate.

Once this formula is in place, you have an objective format by which you can hold individuals on the team accountable for what they have accomplished and how they have accomplished it. Follow this recipe for your semiannual or annual performance review. But once again, you as the leader must be an example and a role model, or the plan will ring hollow to the ears of every member of your team.

Then, every chance you have, get up on your soapbox and reiterate the message; identify which values you want to see your team demonstrate, tell them what the values "look like" by telling them *stories* that show the values in action, and tell them why these particular leadership values are so important: that's the what, how, and why of ICE. Every platform chance you have, every group session, big or small, remind the team of your expectations when it comes to performance and behaviors.

If you have defined the mission, the objectives, and the behaviors you expect, and if you are modeling what you want from the members of the organization, then you have earned the right to speak to them about it, and that is exactly what you should do. No one should have any doubt about what you expect the organization to accomplish and how you believe they should behave as they are accomplishing the goals and objectives.

I mentioned earlier that performance reviews are one of the special opportunities to build our ICE muscles. Actually, I think if the performance review is done correctly, it is the most intense workout a boss or supervisor can have. As a leader, when you have finished your performance review with one of your direct reports, those muscles should be sore and burning and you should be exhausted. I experienced this firsthand on the receiving end of a review in January 2004.

Up until this time and especially since the early nineties when I moved into a senior management position, I never really experienced a thorough, structured performance review. As I mentioned in this chapter, I have worked for people who were terrific mentors, but I must admit for whatever reason they were not really interested in doing these reviews in a thorough, structured manner. In Jim Butler's case it was probably because we were so close that he felt that he was providing the necessary feedback on a regular basis, and that was probably true. From the receiving end, my experience was that performance reviews were either quick meetings of fifteen to thirty minutes between me and my boss simply to highlight what kind of year I had had, or they were nonexistent. So I modeled their behavior, and that is exactly how I conducted the reviews of my direct reports.

All that changed in January 2004 when I had my first formal review with my new boss, Chris Viehbacher. Chris came to the United States and became president of GSK, U.S. in 2003. Before that time, he was president of GSK, Europe. From the first time I met him, I really liked him. He appeared to be engaging, thoughtful, and knowledgeable about the business. Chris seemed to care about our people because he was willing to listen and learn, and all of the above proved to be true. I have worked for a number of presidents in this organization, and I can say confidently that no one practiced the ICE values of leadership better than Chris Viehbacher.

On the day of my first performance review with Chris, scheduled for 11 a.m., I was anticipating that I would be finished by about

11:30, leaving me time for a four-mile run, a quick lunch, and then back to work. I arrived at his office right before my scheduled time. At eleven o'clock sharp, Chris invited me into his office. Being the son of German parents, Chris believes in punctuality; as he likes to say, "In Germany, the trains run on time."

We sat down at his conference table, and for the next two hours he reviewed with me his perception of the company's performance, my organization's performance, and my individual contributions. His comments, though, were not limited only to objective business metrics; he also spent quite a bit of time reflecting on how the organization's culture and spirit had changed during the year. He listened to my own evaluation of how the company had performed and how he had performed. Finally, he wanted to know from me what we could do better as a company and what I could do better in the coming year.

When we were finished, I thanked him for the review, and instead of just shaking hands we actually hugged. It was a very meaningful event for me. I had to go for a brief walk by myself because that review was both exhausting and emotional, and I needed to collect myself before I returned to my office. My review with Chris was ICE at its best. He was honest and courageous in that he gave me feedback that he believed was the truth, notwithstanding the difficulty of sharing with me those areas of my work he had decided needed improvement.

But he was empathetic, too, in that he delivered his messages in a way that showed me he cared about my feelings and was interested in my perceptions of how things were going. It left me with a feeling of respect for him because I could see that Chris was leading from the sweet spot: as I said in chapter 7, empathetic leaders *do* care, but they also *do* lead. This point of balance in empathy is the sweet spot. In my performance review meeting that January day I had just found another role model who could teach me to lead from that dynamic point of balance, the center of percussion for home runs I might find along the bat, the dynamic balance of care and strength.

The next time I met with my direct reports, I shared with them the thoroughness, style, and quality of Chris's performance review with me. I also let them know how positive emotionally and motivating from a business standpoint those *two* hours were to me. Since that day four years ago, each review I have with my direct reports has been a carbon copy of the manner in which Chris reviewed me that day, and I am proud to say that my direct reports have chosen to do likewise with their own staffs.

However, none of us is hanging around here in warm-up suits, sipping cocktails by a roaring fire, and patting each other on the back. *Au contraire!* We are aware that the ICE muscles can turn to fat overnight, that they can atrophy and wither away unless we continue to hold onto our awareness of the performance of great leadership when we see it, unless we talk about it to our people whenever we get a chance, and unless we practice it every day incrementally, like Tiger Woods does. And you, too—don't languish with your peers in a self-congratulatory or complacent mood. Go to the gym and get a good workout of your ICE muscles. I've found that it's the only way to go.

You should come to work every day with
the intention of delivering real value
for the company.

GEORGE MORROW

Chapter Nine

———

WHERE'S THE BEEF?

$\mathcal{B}$ack in 1984, a funny and clever advertising campaign was conducted by one of the national hamburger chains. We saw it on TV over and over again—the "Where's the beef?" ad. The goal of the campaign was for the sponsor to differentiate itself in the highly undifferentiated world of the fast-food hamburger industry. Their core message was to belittle the size of the major competitor's beef patty. It was a classic and, I might add, a very successful piece of advertising.

A character named Clara, the actress Clara Peller playing a crotchety old lady, would look quizzically across the counter when the competing company's server handed her the hamburger she had ordered. She would look at it. She would then pause, scrunch up her face, look at him square in the eyes, and bark, "Where's the beef?"

"Where's the beef?" caught on so quickly and so effectively that it wasn't long before that little slogan was used routinely when people wanted to know the gist of a situation, the point of it all—underneath the jargon and spin. It quickly spread into the business world, where even today it enjoys remarkable staying power. More than twenty years later, you still hear people using that phrase when they want to know the bottom line of a particular deal or issue.

Having spent a lot of time in this book writing about leadership values and behaviors, I expect you also may be wondering "Where's the beef?" Just like Clara, by now you might have your face all scrunched up staring over the counter at me, wondering what my ICE model means when it comes to creating real, tangible value or real beef in your corporation.

In any type of leadership, but especially in business leadership and even more specifically in public companies with the dreaded quarterly report card, "Where's the beef?" is all about delivering value for your company. Every quarter, you have to report publicly to your shareholders, employees, auditors, and regulators about the current health and future prognosis of your organization. You have no place to hide. Everything is exposed. That's just part of life in publicly traded companies, especially today in the wake of corporate scandals like Enron and in the demanding reporting environment of the Sarbanes-Oxley Law.

So where *is* the beef? One obvious measure of it is the financial performance of the company. For leaders in any organization where private equity funds and public investors bet boatloads of dollars on the people, products, strategies, and tactics of your organization, "Where's the beef?" is about delivering return on investment to the millions who have placed a bet on your company. Whether they are individual investors who play the stock market as a means of enhancing their own net worth, or institutional investors who have been entrusted to invest money from 401(k) and pension plans for various organizations, all of them want the same thing. They want to see quarterly and annual profit growth. For leaders of publicly traded companies, the primary job every day is to come to work thinking about new and better ways to improve profits and to deliver a positive return to investors.

This is distinctly different from simply managing processes. Leaders should not spend a great deal of time micromanaging administrative activities. Instead, leaders should spend the bulk of their time thinking creatively about market opportunities, competitive weaknesses, and strategic alliances that, once exploited, will result in real material value for their shareholders and for their organizations.

That doesn't mean you should be soft on management control. Obviously, improving profits and good management are not mutually exclusive, but given the chance to paint on a new canvas versus touching up the old one, I opt for working with my team on creative opportunities, leaving the touch-up work for others entrusted with those important responsibilities.

I have a simple litmus test for whether a leader is creating enough financial value for the corporation: Can people say that as leaders we are way *overpaid* for what we do on a day-to-day basis and that we are way *underpaid* for the material value that we provide to our organization? In other words, it is not about sweat and muscle. It's all about thinking and optimization. One effective creative thought in any highly profitable industry like pharmaceuticals is priceless for its operational efficiencies, not to mention its payback to shareholders.

In late 2005 it became apparent to me that the exceptional growth of the Neurohealth business unit that I lead would decrease in late 2008 and that the drop would continue in 2009. This would occur as a result of the loss of patent protection for our two flagship medicines, Lamictal and Requip. In addition, new neurology and psychiatry medicines from our research labs would probably not become commercially available until after 2009. For a division that had produced a compounded annual growth rate of approximately 40 percent from 2001 through 2005, this was a daunting and unacceptable situation.

There was just no way we could sit around and let this happen. We had to find a solution—something that would create value for the division and for the company. It was a leadership, "Where's-the-beef?" litmus test for me and the commercial leader of the Neurohealth business unit, Diane Tulp. By the way, Diane is, in my opinion, one of the best leaders of sales and marketing that I have ever seen, and I have seen my share.

So Diane and I conducted a series of one-on-one meetings in order to assess the situation and formulate a strategy. It did not take us long to decide that we should pursue every external opportunity to in-license medicines from other companies that would hit the sweet spot of neurology or psychiatry commercial attractiveness. In other words, we wanted to find new medicines that were on the doorstep of being submitted to the FDA for approval to market in the United States, also known as Phase III.

And we wanted to find new medicines that would be prescribed predominantly by neurologists and psychiatrists.

In the pharmaceutical industry, many times very small start-up companies find a technology that allows them to relatively quickly and inexpensively navigate a medicine to approval. The only problem is that these smaller organizations, which consist mostly of scientists, do not have the commercial strength or capabilities to market those medicines themselves, especially in large, competitive markets like the United States. They have the asset, and we have the sales and marketing expertise—a match made in heaven!

The first thing Diane and I decided was that we would get our business development people to run a search of all late-phase medicines that could have application in neurology and psychiatry. We were looking for late-stage medicines that treat diseases such as epilepsy, multiple sclerosis, ALS or Lou Gehrig's disease, restless-leg syndrome, neuropathic pain, schizophrenia, bipolar depression, and psychosis, just to name a few. Then we would prioritize the candidates that emerged from that search as either "major-league" or "minor-league" players.

Once we had the list and the prioritization completed, we could begin the process of getting out and knocking on the doors of companies with prospective medicines we thought could be attractive. We decided that we would take an active role in this process or, as I like to say, "buy airline tickets so that we could go shopping and wave our corporate charge card in the faces of the CEOs of these small companies."

That is exactly what we did. In early 2006 we traveled to

New York City to meet the president and the chief executive of a relatively small, publicly traded biotechnology company. They had a medicine in late-stage development for the treatment of neurologically related diseases that we believed would be a nice fit for our Neurohealth division. Upon arrival we introduced ourselves to their president and to their CEO, and then Diane and I did our best to persuade them that Glaxo's experience, commercial strength, and track record of success should be key drivers in their decision to partner with GSK; we pitched our capabilities with passion and conviction.

They were accommodating and receptive. They listened closely to our presentations, and it appeared to me from their comments and body language that they agreed with our position. We believed that GSK was the company that could do the best job of commercializing their medicine. That's not to say they did not question us or challenge us on a number of issues. But we were well prepared to answer their questions and address their challenges. We did, however, face a very significant hurdle: GSK was late to this game. We assumed the company was already being courted by several major pharmaceutical companies, some of whom were direct competitors of GSK.

So Diane and I decided to put on the full-court press, meaning we took a direct interest in all aspects of this potential deal. Regardless of whether it was an internal process like deal structure or an external process like negotiating the terms, she and I were present and actively involved. Finally, after about eight months, we were down to the wire.

Their CEO called and asked Diane and me to come out to his

company to present GSK and our commercial capabilities to his board. Their CEO and their president were sold on our ability to commercialize their medicine, but they were even more sold on our passion and belief in the commercial capabilities of our organization. The CEO wanted his board to see that passion firsthand. In late January 2007 we went to their headquarters for their board meeting, and we presented our case with conviction and passion. And in early February we inked the deal!

Financial metrics are very important, and they are certainly very measurable. Adding value, however, is not only about financial return. As a leader, your first job is to deliver financial results, but earnings per share, P/E ratios, bonus payouts, revenues, and profits are not the only measure of a leader's success. Another important area where leaders should distinguish themselves in an accountable way is building an organization that attracts and retains good people. This, too, is easily measured.

Just like financial scorecards, other scorecards measure a leader's ability to build a stimulating organization and foster an organizational culture where people feel connected and committed. These scorecards are referred to as Employee Satisfaction Surveys. They consist of a series of questions that query the employee to identify on a scale how satisfied they are with such things as the organization's mission, vision, culture, strategic direction, and compensation and rewards program. You have probably filled out many of these yourself. This instrument is a proxy for measuring how effective the company's leadership is in creating a fertile and effective work environment.

Although I love the concept of surveying employees, I despise the name, Employee Satisfaction Survey. Think about it. How uninspiring and lukewarm is the word "satisfied"? It screams "average," "C-plus," or "normal." Let me ask you: how many times have you gone to an Oscar-nominated movie, seen a Broadway play, or eaten dinner at a five-star restaurant, and then said, "That satisfied me." No! You probably said something like, "That was terrific!" "That was a wonderful experience!" or "Wow! I really loved it, and I want to go back!"

So I suggest we set the same standards for measuring the organizational environment and organizational culture that we lead. We should allow our critics, the people in our organization, the license to provide us with a no-holds-barred Emotional Report Card about our performance.

In the two organizations I currently lead, I utilize a phrase that describes this measurement standard. I call it "stickiness," and all I want to know is how sticky is my organization for the people who work in it. I want these organizations to be places where our people truly understand that they have the liberty to leave. But I also want to make it difficult for them to leave because we have created an environment where our people experience a workplace that is challenging, productive, meaningful, rewarding, and fun. The result should be that when other internal or external organizations attempt to recruit our people, they find it difficult because our people like where they work and recognize the effort we put into developing this sticky environment.

If I were some human resources guru, which I am not, I would change the name of the Employee Satisfaction Survey to the Employee Love Survey. It would measure the degree to which people love being a part of our organization. It would measure their affinity for the company, and it would quantify how sticky we have made our organization for the individuals who work in it. Instead of using stars or numbers to rate it, I would use *hearts*.

Within my two divisions, my direct reports Diane Tulp, John Delgiorno, Dan Long, Jack Fish, Anne Faul, and Bill Leonard not only understand this concept of stickiness, but they also buy into it in a big way. When I step back from the day-to-day activities, I see people leading in their departments and producing terrific results in their challenging environments. Yet, when I talk to our folks—and it doesn't matter where they sit on the corporate totem pole—I hardly ever hear negativity or grumbling. I rarely detect complacency or dissatisfaction in their voices. Instead, I consistently hear excitement for accepting new challenges, and I sense real appreciation for the opportunities that they have been given.

Voluntary turnover in our two areas is virtually nonexistent. That's not because opportunities do not surface. In our business and in a company this large, new opportunities and exciting promotions are the norm. Turnover is rare because we have created a culture of stickiness in our organization. Simply put, our people want to stay here.

This does not happen accidentally. The stickiness in our organization is a function of the leadership team's buy-in to the concept of creating a productive yet enjoyable workplace. Let me share one example.

In the Managed Care Division, I have a department called the Pharmacy Benefit Management Team. We refer to them simply as the PBM Team, a relatively small department of nine people, but each one makes a significant impact on the success of GSK's business. Our PBM Team negotiates contracts with four major pharmacy benefit-management companies, otherwise known as PBMs, which manage prescription-drug coverage for the large, Fortune 500 employers and major health-care plans throughout the country. There are four PBM companies that dominate this marketplace—Medco, Caremark, Express Scripts, and Med Impact—and these companies actually define which medicines will be covered and to what extent they will be covered. In total, these four corporations influence the prescription drug benefit for almost 150 million Americans.

This is how it works: If you are employed by a large company and your company provides a menu of health-care options, like self-insurance, indemnity health care, or managed care, it is very likely that the prescription portion of your benefit is outsourced to one of the above-mentioned companies. Your company has probably contracted with that PBM to provide you with a prescription drug program that balances broad access to many medicines with a cost-effective offering for your company. In other words, through the PBM, your company wants you to have a broad choice of medicines, but they also want someone to negotiate a reasonable price that they will pay for those medicines. Your employer in this situation has empowered the PBM to create a drug formulary or list of medicines with varying co-pays that will be paid by the employee, based on the value proposition (efficacy, safety, and cost of each medicine) in its respective therapeutic class.

Now take a look inside your purse or wallet. You probably have a prescription drug card. If so, the odds are that the PBM that manages your benefit is one of the large PBM companies.

So now you go to your doctor. It is allergy season, late summer or early spring, and you are sneezing like crazy. Your doctor writes a prescription for a type of medicine called an intranasal steroid. Many intranasal steroids are on the market, both generic and branded medicines. You take your prescription for the intranasal steroid as well as your prescription card to your local pharmacy. The pharmacist enters the information from the prescription your doctor has written as well as the information from your card into their computer system. The pharmacy's computer then immediately messages the PBM that manages your plan's prescription benefit in order to figure out how much your company is willing to pay and how much you are required to pay for the medicine that your doctor has prescribed.

The amount you will pay is called the co-pay. Generally there are three tiers of co-pays. Tier-one, usually about five to ten dollars, is for the generic products in that class of medicines (in this example, the class is intranasal steroids). Tier-two is typically about twenty-five to thirty-five dollars for the preferred, branded product. Branded products are those medicines that do not yet have a generic equivalent. Tier-three is customarily reserved for the nonpreferred branded product, and it is about forty to fifty dollars.

In our business, our target is to get all of our medicines into tier-two status. That is a desirable and profitable position since it provides us with economically preferred positioning versus tier-three, and since we really don't attempt to compete with generic products, those in tier-one. The bottom line is if our medicines are listed in the second tier, we feel very confident that once a physician prescribes that medicine, then that is the medicine the patient will receive.

So PBMs can dramatically influence our market opportunity. Subsequently, our PBM Team plays a very important role in developing strategic offerings and contracts across our entire portfolio of medicines that ensures second-tier access for our medicines through four companies representing more than half of the U.S. population. Obviously, this is no small task. Four PBMs, a super oligopoly, provide consolidated buying power for this population, and the reality is that our products compete in highly competitive therapeutic classes where there may be little clinical difference among branded products. Many times, it just comes down to price or the contracted rebate we offer to the health plans or employers through these PBMs.

If we lose one of the PBMs for an important product and that PBM puts our product in the third tier, we could lose a market opportunity for almost 60 million people. Needless to say, our PBM Team works in an environment of intense pressure and competition. The leader of this team is Bill Leonard, who reports to me and has done so for the better part of twenty years.

I first met Bill in 1985. He was a brand-new sales rep, and I was one of his sales trainers. Both of us came from the Northeast. Bill was from Long Island, and quite frankly both of us enjoyed a common habit—the attraction of a nice adult beverage after the trials and tribulations of a hard day at work. So after a long day of Glaxo product training at the North Raleigh Hilton, it would not be unusual to find Bill and me bellying up to the bar to take the edge off an intense day of training and to discuss common interests like sports, politics, or the latest escapades of the New York or Philly organized-crime families. We really hit it off, and have ever since.

In 1988, when I finally received approval to expand our managed care department, Bill was one of the first people to raise his hand and volunteer for service. It was Bill in the Northeast; Chris Carney, another great friend, in the Midwest; and Carl Pepe in the New England states, just to name a few. That was the crew that first saw the handwriting on the wall and came forward to seize this opportunity to help our company address a new, influential market and, quite frankly, to help themselves seize a market opportunity to turbocharge their careers. In the pharmaceutical business we were like the *Niña*, the *Pinta*, and the *Santa Maria* setting sail on a journey to a new world.

And as I said earlier, Bill is still with me today. Since that time in 1988, Bill Leonard has continuously worked in my organization. He has had numerous opportunities to do other things, both inside and outside of GSK, but for twenty years he has resisted recruitment and has been a very loyal and most productive member of my team.

But Bill has taken that loyalty and production, that "Where's the beef?" mentality, and driven it into the PBM organization that he now runs. His people are on the line for the tier-two positioning of GSK medicines in the four big Pharmacy Benefit Management companies that I have described. Bill's crew manages billions of dollars of GSK's business annually. If their strategy fails and any of these PBMs restricts one of our key medicines, it could have a serious material effect on GSK. It is a tough, competitive environment.

So even though Bill's people are under a lot of pressure, almost no one voluntarily leaves his organization. Let me set the record straight. Since our merger with SmithKline back in 2001, only one person has left Bill's team voluntarily, and that was due to retirement from GSK. Let me also add that within our company there is no market segment in managed care that has better access for our medicines than the PBM segment.

Bill has delivered the beef both in terms of financial value for our shareholders and real stickiness for his people. If she could see Bill today, Clara would be so proud, unscrunching her skeptical look, paying for her burger, and taking it to her table without a single complaint! She might even add an order of fries.

Our deepest fear is not that we are inadequate.

Our deepest fear is that we are powerful beyond measure.

It is our light, not our darkness, that most frightens us.

MARIANNE WILLIAMSON

Chapter Ten

———

PEER CEILING

One of the most important lessons I have learned about the impact of one's confidence on professional development did not happen in the offices or conference rooms of my business environ-ment. It happened much earlier and in a much different setting. It was a lesson I learned the hard way from the hardwood floors of the basketball courts I played on during my youth.

I, like almost everyone else from the sixties and seventies in the Philadelphia area, was totally into two things: listening to Motown music and playing competitive basketball. Philly was then and probably will always be a city that provides a great basketball environment and produces even greater basketball players. Back in the late sixties and early seventies, basketball was at its apex in the City of Brotherly Love.

We had incredible professional players like Wilt Chamberlain, Chet Walker, and Hal Greer; legendary college coaches such as Jack Ramsey, Harry Litwack, and Jack Kraft; and we had doubleheaders every Wednesday and Saturday night during the basketball season at the historic Palestra, the official home court of the University of Pennsylvania and the unofficial home court for the "Big Five." The Philadelphia 76ers had come off their first National Basketball Association (NBA) championship in 1967, and the "Big Five," consisting of St. Joe, Villanova, Temple, LaSalle, and Penn, was one of the most competitive leagues in college basketball.

All of my buddies—people like Phil Martelli, who today is the head basketball coach at St. Joe and one of the best coaches in college basketball—were totally obsessed with this sport. It seemed as if we spent every waking minute playing the game, watching it on television, listening to it on the radio, or simply talking about it. Most of the time, however, we played it. In the summer, we would convene at a tiny outdoor court in Lansdowne around ten o'clock in the morning and by noon, it was constant full-court basketball games until about four o'clock in the afternoon. We called these games "Winners," meaning the winning team would keep playing until they lost. The first ten to arrive would get the first game. By twelve o'clock there were usually about fifteen to twenty guys ready to play.

The remainder would call out "Winners" and wait their turn. So if you lost, the team that had called "Winners" would play and your team would sit out. Kind of like a round-robin, elimination tournament. This would go on all day. Then we would go home, eat dinner, and return to the court around six o'clock and do it all over again. That is, unless we were playing in some evening summer league.

If it was winter, and we were in full basketball season, we would practice for about two hours four to five days per week, and we would usually have one or two games to play as well. That crowded schedule, however, did not preclude our playing weekend pickup games on decent winter days at our little outdoor court, or from finding some indoor gym to play in on inclement days whether we were welcome or not. I can assure you, for guys like Phil and me it was all basketball, all the time.

My fascination with basketball and with the processes I've described were the catalysts for honing my skills and becoming a pretty good player. I could shoot well, I could handle the ball, and since I was pretty quick, I could play solid defense. I was also very fortunate in that during my most formative years, roughly ages ten through thirteen, I had the benefit of being tutored by very competent coaches. They were true basketball mentors—people like Tom Gallagher, Pete O'Keefe, and John Steele, who not only knew the game very well, but also understood how to teach it, especially to young players. So by the time I was in my last year of grade school, I could hold my own against any other guard in our league.

But the real basketball litmus test was yet to come—eight months later when I tried out for the freshman basketball team in high school, Monsignor Bonner. Bonner was and is today a very big high school with a very big basketball reputation. Our grade-school league consisted of about fifteen schools that were feeder schools into Bonner. That meant that about 120 to 140 eager kids would try out for Bonner's freshman team each year, but only 12 to 15 were selected. It was very competitive. If you made that team, it meant serious bragging rights back in the neighborhood.

As soon as the season ended at St. Philomena's (my grade school), I set my goal and developed my plan for making Bonner's squad. Throughout the spring, summer, and into fall, I never took a break from playing and practicing basketball. I was at the Lansdowne court every day playing in those pickup games. I played in summer leagues. I worked every day with my eighth-grade coach, Tom Gallagher. I did my "Pete Maravich Homework" ball-handling drills. I ran wind sprints and even completed a one-mile run each night to build my stamina. My plan was that nothing was going to stop me from giving it my personal best effort to make that team.

When my family went on our annual two-week vacation to the South Jersey Shore, every day I went to a basketball court located about one mile from our house. Each morning after my dad returned from Mass around 7:30 a.m.—he went every day—he would drive me to the court, where I would stay, play, and practice until he picked me up around noon.

During this entire eight-month training process while I was working on my game, there was one nagging concern I had to overcome. People around me, especially my basketball friends, kept telling me that I had virtually no chance of making the team. Since they were older than I, and since most of them had experienced their own disappointment in trying out for and not making Bonner's freshman team, they had firsthand experience of how competitive it was to get on that roster. They had competed with me and against me, so they were very aware of my abilities. They believed that my chances were limited not because of my skills but because of my size.

Even though they whispered their negative thoughts to me, I refused to listen. I turned a deaf ear to those naysayers and focused entirely on following my plan. As I mentioned, nothing was going to stop me from executing my plan to give it my personal best effort. I just had to give it my best shot! And that is exactly what I did. I adopted this mind-set: "It is entirely up to me to do everything I can to make it." I knew that I had no control over my height, but I also knew that I could control what I could do with my skills and my determination.

When it was time for tryouts in October 1969, I had my game in top condition. My shooting and ball-handling mechanics were in pristine shape, and my physical conditioning was excellent. Additionally, I was mentally prepared. When I stepped onto the court for that first day of tryouts, I was ready to go. And it's a good thing that I was!

Day One of tryouts was very intense. It was divided into two sessions in order to accommodate approximately 120 eager kids, all of whom believed they had a serious chance to make the team. The process was simple. Each of the coaches took a different station along the eight half-court areas. Then we were divided into groups of 6 to 8 players. First they just watched while we warmed up, then they blew their whistles to begin a series of one-on-one games. All of us knew it was showtime. Guards played against guards, forwards played against forwards, and centers played against centers. The selection process was cut-and-dried. With few exceptions, it was like the Roman gladiators in the Coliseum. If you lost, you were gone, you were "dead." If you won, you were invited back for Day Two.

Day Two was no different except instead of two "gladiator sessions" of one-on-one games, there was just one. Once again it was win or go home. I made this all-important cut!

After these two pressure-packed days, the coaches had a more manageable group of 30-some talented tryouts whose skills they could now take some quality time to evaluate thoroughly. The one-on-one half-court games were replaced with hours of basketball drills and five-on-five full-court games. Over a period of about two weeks, our coaches analyzed our individual skills and our teamwork ability. Little by little they were honing the number of tryouts down through a selection process until finally they had their 14 players and what they believed was a highly competitive team. More than 120 players had tried out and only 14 would survive. Sounds like a reality show on today's TV, doesn't it?

The night before the final cut was announced, I hardly slept a wink. I tossed and turned. I felt confident that I had done everything I could to prepare, and I believed I had played very well throughout the two-week tryout process. I knew I had the skills to make the team. It was apparent to me that I could shoot and handle the ball as well as, if not better than, most of the other kids at tryouts, but I kept thinking, *What if my friends are right? What if I'm just too small and don't have the physical makeup to earn a position on such a competitive team?*

Finally, although it seemed like an eternity, the next morning arrived. I quickly got dressed and almost ran the full mile to school. In the hallway outside our gym on a small corkboard there was a note that read, "The following freshman players are to report to the gym at 4:00 p.m. to get their uniforms." Below that note was the roster list, and on that list appeared my name! Wow, what a feeling!

At four o'clock I was front and center in the gym. Our head coach Dick Bernhardt along with his assistants and our equipment managers walked out onto the court with boxes containing fourteen Bonner home and away uniforms. Bernhardt sat us on the bench, and after congratulating us, he reviewed his expectations and rules for behavior. Then came the moment of truth when he individually handed out our uniforms. I was so excited that I could barely breathe.

The moral of that story is not in the determination I showed during the eight months before my freshman-year basketball tryouts. More important is to contrast this story of success against what happened in my sophomore-, junior-, and senior-year tryouts. Even though I was successful in making the freshman team through my ability, preparation, and belief in myself, I was unsuccessful in making my high-school team in any of those subsequent years because I stopped believing in my own ability. I believe you learn your best lessons not through wins, but through failures.

It wasn't because my skills had deteriorated; in fact, they had improved. Physically I was getting bigger and stronger. It wasn't because I tried less than I had before. I utilized the same workout and practice plan that had served me so well during my freshman year.

I failed to make those teams because I started to listen to and believe the people around me, especially my teammates who were telling me, "Steve, you were really lucky to make the freshman team, but there is no way you can ever make the junior varsity or varsity teams. You're good, man, but you're just too short!"

Unlike my freshman year when I had turned a deaf ear to my friends, now I was listening with long, tall rabbit ears to my teammates, taking it all in. By the way, these were the same people with whom I competed for a spot on the varsity and junior varsity rosters. I was allowing my competition to influence my confidence and my belief in myself. Serious doubt started to creep into my mind. I began to believe perhaps they were right; perhaps these teams were out of reach for me. *Perhaps I should just be satisfied with having made the freshman team*, I thought. The result was three consecutive years of getting to the last cut and then feeling the deep disappointment of not making it. Looking at that posted list outside our gym and finding my name absent from it, then attending games as a paying spectator and not a worthy participant were so discouraging.

I had allowed my teammates from my freshman team—the same people who were my colleagues against opposing teams but who also were internal competitors when it came to playing positions for our junior varsity and varsity teams—to influence my thinking. I had allowed *them* to establish a perceived limit or ceiling in my own mind of my chances for success. Unfortunately, I bought into what they were selling me. This in turn resulted in a level of acceptance of or satisfaction with the status quo, what I had already accomplished—being a player on the freshman team.

I have a name for this self-limiting complacency: I call it the *peer ceiling*. It happened to me in high school basketball, and through that valuable lesson I learned that I would never again let any of my peers influence my own perception of what I could accomplish. The phenomenon of the peer ceiling is very similar to one known in corporations as the glass ceiling, which establishes an artificial and unfair perceptual limit of how far females and minorities can progress in the corporate world. Glass ceilings result in thinking throughout the corporation that accepts a current level of success and stifles growth and ability to progress. It implies, even when not stated outright, "We all understand that this is as much as you can achieve, but it's pretty much, so I'm sure that you're grateful for it." Thankfully, most corporations are addressing this unfair limit to competition through succession planning that incorporates diversity strategies.

Colleagues in the corporate world are not unlike teammates in the sports world. When it comes to outside opponents, everyone tries to work together to defeat the competition. Yet when it comes to internal opportunities, many times it is every man or woman for him- or herself. And that is okay. It creates normal and healthy competition, both externally and internally. It builds character and it builds skills, if everyone plays fairly. The process of going after opportunities deteriorates, however, when members of the team or peers in an organization either consciously or unconsciously attempt to create a psychological advantage for themselves. Make no mistake about it; it can and does happen.

Building peer ceilings is an effective method of creating psychological advantage. Your own corporate colleagues try to establish a perception that you don't have the "size" or "physical makeup" to progress to the next corporate level—the junior varsity or varsity team. Simple and subtle comments like "You need an MBA," or "You don't have the varied experiences," or "You've never worked outside the United States" are just three examples of limiting statements I have heard many times during my career. I put them in the same category as "Don't you think you're too small, Steve, to make the freshman team?"

The truth is that many of your colleagues are pursuing the same corporate opportunities as you. They, too, are looking for that next position, or that roster spot on the junior varsity or varsity corporate team, and if you allow them to create a stifling self-perception about your own qualifications, then you have opened up a crack in your psychological armor. When that happens, it results in nagging self-questioning or self-doubt about your own abilities to progress to the next level. At that point, you have created a peer ceiling in your own mind and you have limited your chances for growth and success.

Limits of growth and progression have been established, and your colleagues have gained a big psychological advantage. They have caused you to compromise your confidence and close your mind. Upon his release from prison, Nelson Mandela said that we also can limit ourselves because of a very basic human fear:

> Our deepest fear is not that we are inadequate. Our deepest fear is that we are powerful beyond measure. It is our light, not our darkness, that most frightens us. We ask ourselves, Who am I to be brilliant, gorgeous, talented, fabulous? Actually, who are you *not* to be?

You are a child of God. Your playing small does not serve the world. There is nothing enlightened about shrinking so that other people won't feel insecure around you. We are all meant to shine, as children do. We were born to make manifest the glory of God that is within us. It's not just in some of us; it's in everyone. And as we let our own light shine, we unconsciously give other people permission to do the same. As we are liberated from our own fear, our presence automatically liberates others.

From Marianne Williamson's
Return to Love, Harper Collins, 1992

My friend Pat Croce tells a great story in his motivational talks about one of his heroes, Harry Houdini. There's no way I can do justice to this story through writing about it. You really need to hear Pat tell it in his own words and in his own inspirational manner. But let me give it the old college try.

Houdini, as you probably know, was one of the greatest escape artists of all times, not to mention a world-class self-promoter. In this story, a small village in France has built a new jail. The warden boasts that the jail is physically so tight that even the Great Houdini cannot escape from it. The challenge goes out, and it's not long before it gets to Houdini, who naturally accepts it. He crosses the Atlantic, arrives in the village, and readies himself to take on the challenge.

On the day of the event, Houdini is heavily escorted to the jail site. The press and spectators are there in large numbers. Once inside the prison walls, Houdini is then stripped completely naked, shackled at the wrists and ankles, and led into one of the newly built cells. He is placed inside the cell, and then the jailer shuts the door and turns the lock in a peculiar manner. Houdini is left alone to attempt his escape.

The jailer and the warden leave the area. Houdini then coughs up a small eggshell-like casing, which he swallowed shortly before entering the cell. Inside the casing is a tiny pick which he uses to free himself quickly from the handcuffs and ankle shackles. He gets to work on the cell lock.

Typically, it takes Houdini about five minutes to pick any lock, so he feels certain that this will be a piece of cake. Houdini kneels down so that his ear is right against the cell lock and he starts working on it. He listens intently to the sounds of the tumblers as he slowly turns the lock. Five minutes go by and nothing happens. Ten minutes, then thirty, then one hour and still no progress. After two gruesome hours, soaked in perspiration and completely exhausted, Houdini rises and is ready to give up and admit defeat.

He leans against the cell door to rest and think, when unexpectedly the cell door swings wide open! You see, the jailer had never locked the door—on purpose! The door was only "locked" in Houdini's mind. It was his mental mind-set, or as Pat says, a "locked mind" not a locked door, that had almost defeated him.

The dynamics of working in a corporation are not much different than the dynamics of playing for a basketball team or for any sports team. That is why so many analogies to sports are applied to the corporate world. Think about it. Both are very hierarchical. The basketball team has its coach and starting five. The corporation has its chief executive and key talent. Both the team and corporation establish goals, mission, behaviors, rewards, and recognition. Neither one could succeed without a balance of solid teamwork and individual performance. These are just a couple of the similarities between the corporate world and the sport I still love.

I have shared my personal story about trying out for high-school basketball and Pat Croce's striking story about the Great Houdini because both establish vivid images that would serve you well to recall as you rise in the corporate world. I have seen that peer ceilings and psychological gamesmanship many times result in closing one's mind to opportunities for growth and success.

So the next time a nice promotion or coveted position opens up, and one or two of your colleagues suggest that you are not qualified for the position, remember Pat's Houdini story or just remember this: even if you are challenged in one way or another, you can still make the team. It's not the size of the dog in the fight. It is the size of the fight in the dog. So don't let your apparent size keep you off the team, and don't let a locked mind keep you from realizing your aspirations and your dreams.

There is a certain degree of satisfaction in
having the courage to admit one's errors. It not only
clears up the air of guilt and defensiveness, but often
helps solve the problem created by the error.

DALE CARNEGIE

Chapter Eleven

ICE STORMS

$\mathcal{L}$iving in North Carolina for as many years as I have has given me wonderful opportunities to see and enjoy its incredible natural beauty. We have eight months of temperate weather, usually around seventy to eighty degrees. Most evenings we enjoy beautiful Carolina blue skies and crystal-clear starlit nights. Our coast is natural and clean. In my opinion, there is no doubt that we have the finest collection of golf courses anywhere in the world. I mean, who could find fault with Pinehurst? Okay, maybe Pebble Beach.

But like everywhere else, we also have our share of natural disasters. If you live in California, it is earthquakes. If you reside in Texas or Oklahoma, it is tornadoes. If your home is in upstate New York or in New England, it is blizzards. If you live in Louisiana or Florida, it is hurricanes. If you live in North Carolina, it is ice storms, and our ice storms can be debilitating, if not disastrous. I mentioned earlier one particular ice storm during the beginning of my career in North Carolina and how it absolutely paralyzed the area.

When our meteorologists tell us that the temperature will hover on the thirty-two-degree freezing line and that there is the threat of precipitation, we know that we should prepare for an ice storm. The first signals are the full parking lots around our supermarkets and the empty shelves inside them. A little colder and we get snow; a little warmer and it is rain. When the conditions are ripe for several hours of continuous sleet or freezing rain, however, we see once again how destructive an ice storm can be to our routine lives.

Central North Carolina with its acres upon acres of tall, thick pine trees is the perfect place for those pellets of ice to land. Once a storm hits our area, normally two to three times each winter, it only takes a couple of hours before the pine trees are totally encrusted in ice and our roads become winding skating rinks. Initially it is stunningly beautiful, almost as though you are inside a piece of Waterford crystal looking outward. The view is spectacular. The roads are shiny. The lawns look like sugar-coated cookies, and the pine trees appear to be giant icicles.

At first, you think the ice storm is just a harmless thing of beauty, but after several hours you realize how dangerous it can be. Those icicle-looking pine trees become overstressed from the weight of the heavy precipitation, and one by one they start to crack and fall. The streets that initially appeared to be harmless skating rinks are transformed into dangerous race tracks for demolition derby. Power lines are torn down by the weight of the ice, and it is not unusual for hundreds of thousands of homes to go without heat or electricity for days. The initial beauty, the first couple of hours of winter wonderland, is overshadowed by the devastation and distraction the storm has created, and you don't fully realize the extent of the damage until the ice has melted.

The same thing happens when you encounter the business equivalent of an ice storm. At first, you are seduced by the beautiful feeling. You perceive you are insulated in a secure environment. But once the temperature rises and the ice thaws, you quickly come to realize the damage the storm has created. During that seductive period, you may fumble an important business deal, compromise a long-standing professional relationship, cause a valuable employee to look for job opportunities externally, or even tarnish your own reputation. The end result is disappointment, disruption, guilt, and shame. All around you trees are falling. Power lines are snapping, and roads are becoming increasingly treacherous.

As I am sure you know by now, integrity, courage, and empathy are leadership values in which I really believe. Throughout my career I have made it my mission not only to practice leadership through these values, but also to share them with anyone who would listen. Yet I know deep down inside, in the corners and crevices of my soul, that if there is one truth about me, it is that I have broken every one of these principles at one time or another in my career. As much as I cherish integrity, courage, and empathy as the essence of great leadership, I know that at times throughout my career I have violated each one of them. I have been the person who has experienced seductive Waterford-like ice storms only to have them melt around me, and once the ice has melted, I have seen firsthand the dramatic effect that compromising my behavior has had on the people who work with me, as well as my own reputation.

Compromising one's principles is normal. We are humans. In the animal kingdom, we have the distinction of possessing reason and the freedom of making individual choices. As I mentioned earlier, through our intellect and free will, we can either make good decisions or bad ones. And one memorable time I violated all three principles in a single act. It was the trifecta, the triple crown of my violating the ICE model. It was my perfect ice storm.

About five years after Glaxo's merger with Burroughs Wellcome, we had decided to restructure our Commercial Operations Unit. Included in that restructuring was our attempt to place much more emphasis and focus on a regional basis for our sales forces. At the time, we had about three thousand sales representatives, and they were divided into about twenty eight regions. Those regions were led by individuals whom we called regional directors (today we call them regional vice presidents). Those twenty-some regional directors reported into four area vice presidents, who reported into me.

As I mentioned, our intent during this restructuring was to ensure greater focus and attention at the regional level, since our belief was that medicine has a regional bias, based on many factors included demographics, climate, population changes, and payor reimbursement just to name a few (e.g., medicine is practiced differently in South Florida than it is in northern Maine). We wanted to build a structure that had better regional accountability. Additionally, we wanted to create an organization where we could divide the massive U.S. pharmaceutical market into more manage-able bite-size chunks.

As part of this restructuring, we approved the principle that our regional directors should live within the regional boundar-ies that housed one of our regional headquarters, which we called hub offices. At the time, we had six hub offices located throughout the United States: Philadelphia, Raleigh, Atlanta, Chicago, Dallas, and Phoenix. So each of those offices would have five to six regional sales directors working in them. We believed this move would facilitate the focus we were looking for, and we thought it should also provide a collegial environment to enhance teamwork and sharing of best practices.

All of this, however, meant that some of our regional direc-tors would need to relocate, since they currently did not reside in the region that was the hub for the regional office. I convened our four area vice presidents at an offsite meeting to review both what we were going to do and how we were going to do it. Once we determined our objectives, we defined our guiding principles as well as the communication plan of notifying those regional directors who would need to relocate.

We were very rigorous in our approach, because we knew that in addition to its impact on our business, we were well aware that this restructuring, complete with the need for some relocations, would have an impact on people's lives. We wanted to make sure that we did all that we could to dot our i's and cross our t's, and we wanted to make sure that we communicated our message consis-tently to anyone who might have to uproot their family and move to a new location.

One such individual was a guy named Sal Paolella, who was the regional director for Glaxo in the New York City region. At this time, Sal resided in Cary, North Carolina, where he worked out of the Raleigh Hub office and commuted to New York about three to four days each week. Given our new direction, however, Sal would be one of the people who would have to relocate since the closest regional office to New York City was in Philadelphia.

Before I share why this was the perfect ice storm and the triple crown of violating the principles of the ICE model, I need to provide a little background about my professional and personal relationship with Sal. Once you read about that, I am sure you will get the picture.

Sal and I go way back to the early 1980s. He was a sales rep for a company named Ross Laboratories, mostly known for their presence in the infant formula business. We both had very similar territories, and although I did not know Sal at the time, another representative from the same area, who knew both Sal and I well, told me that Sal was looking to get out of the formula business, or as he referred to it, "the milkman business," and get into more mainstream pharmaceuticals.

In anticipation of our launch of Zantac, Glaxo was on a hiring spree. Our senior sales managers were encouraging us to recruit externally for good talent, and our company was offering a one-hundred-dollar finders fee to any sales representative who recruited someone into our company. Back then, that was a lot of money, especially when you consider that my first quarterly bonus check was for six dollars and fifty cents. I cashed it at a local delicatessen, and I used it to purchase a six pack of beer. So, when I heard about Sal, I was very keen to meet him and, if appropriate, recruit him to Glaxo.

We met for the first time on a very cold, damp Friday evening in February 1983, one of those nasty winter nights in Philly when you feel like the chill and dampness go right through you. It was an unforgettable screening that my boss asked me to set up, unforgettable because of a number of reasons that I will not go into detail because they could be the entire chapter of another book. Maybe I could title the chapter "Dressing for Success" or "Managing Time." I am sure Sal would agree. That meeting was unforgettable because there was an immediate connection between the two of us and not simply because I knew that Sal would be perfect for Glaxo. There was almost instant chemistry. We are practically the same age (Sal is a little older), we both come from similar Italian upbringings, and we both love sports, especially golf. We are both highly competitive as well as very dedicated. And believe me when I tell you this, we both like to have a lot of fun.

Immediately after the meeting, I phoned my boss and recommended that he should put the full-court press on Sal and that we should hire him as soon as possible, which is exactly what we did. In the early spring of that year Sal accepted a sales position with Glaxo in the Philly district, and as luck would have it, our territories bumped right up against each other. It was the beginning of a very good and long-term professional relationship. It seemed as though from that point forward our friendship grew and our careers paralleled. Shortly after my promotion to the

Training Department to help prepare our reps to sell Zantac, Sal was promoted to the Marketing Department to help prepare our company to market Zantac.

When I moved on to build our Managed Care Department, Sal was promoted to help build our managed care marketing strategies. Actually, his title was manager of therapeutic equivalence and micromarketing. Sal used to joke that he needed extra large business cards just for his title. And all along we both held various leadership positions in Sales and Managed Care as our careers progressed and as we assumed more responsibilities.

Moreover, from a personal relationship perspective, it was the beginning of a very strong friendship that has lasted until today, notwithstanding some bumps in the road along the way. Sal and I as well as our families, including our parents, have done so much together over the years. We have vacationed together. Who could ever forget that week in Hawaii with our wives? We have partied together, and it seemed to me that we went out almost every weekend, especially in the early days. We have played golf regularly together; I will come back to that in a second. And finally, we have watched our beautiful daughters grow up to become terrific young adults. In fact, I am godfather to Sal and Pat's daughter Krista.

I mentioned golf, and it is so important that I expand on it. From that cold damp night at that little diner outside of Philly where I first met Sal until today, we have shared hundreds and hundreds of rounds of competitive golf, as teammates and as opponents. Let me assure you, there is no one with whom I have played golf who is more competitive than Sal. I tell you this because it underscores what Lee Iacocca wrote in his autobiography *Iacocca: An Autobiography* (Bantam Books, 1984).

Iacocca said you can tell the way people perform and conduct themselves in life and in the business by simply watching how they perform and conduct themselves on the golf course. Sal is the poster child for Iacocca's theory. On the course, he is totally focused on winning. He is very tough on his opponents. He rarely concedes anything to anyone. And, most importantly, he is completely honest. Unlike most weekend golfers, he never shaves a stroke or gives himself a putt. He is just like that in life as well as business. He has a competitive drive to win. He forces his competitor to work hard and beat him, when he is playing at the top of his game. Most importantly, he plays the game of life just like he plays the game of golf—with the highest integrity. He just never cheats!

Now that I have set the stage about Sal, and specifically my relationship with him, it should be very easy for you to understand why this could become an ice storm. As Kim Crutchfield, another great friend and a colleague as well, wrote so eloquently in one of the blurbs for this book, "Throwing caution to the wind, he goes against the cliché never mix business with pleasure. instead combining the two almost perfectly. Steve has formed lifelong friendships and built a high-performing organization within GSK.... My professional and personal relationship with Sal coupled with our need to relocate some people created the ideal mix of barometric pressure and air temperature for a bad ice storm."

Here is what happened. Once the four area vice presidents who reported to me and I left our offsite meeting with our decisions and our communication plan, I decided that I would let them do all of the notifications to those regional directors who would need to relocate, and this would happen in two to three weeks. I was going to stay completely out of it, notwithstanding that I knew that Sal and his family would be impacted. I was inside that piece of Waterford crystal, seduced by its beauty. I should have realized right then and there that I was in the center of an ice storm. Instead of basking in the glory of the frosty beauty, I should have paid attention to those ice pellets hitting me in the head!

On the surface, one could justify that this could be the right thing to do, but deep down inside I knew it was wrong. It was gnawing at me that I would remain silent over the next three weeks and that I would let one of my area VP's handle this tough job. It was also gnawing at me that I was not going to face up to the task of telling one of my best friends what he needed to hear—from me! I was taking corporate cover at a time when, as Kim said, I should have been "throwing caution to the wind."

After a few weeks, the notifications went out. I knew they went out because I approved the date and the content of the notices. Another ten to fourteen days went by, and I did not hear a word from Sal. I knew something was wrong. We usually talked or saw each other two to three times each week. Finally, Sal called and asked me to meet him for a beer at a local watering hole near our homes. We met, and unlike thousands of other times when we got together, including our very first meeting, this time the air felt thick with tension. I was so uncomfortable that I could hardly look Sal in the eyes. He on the other hand, appeared to be downright angry. As he shared with me, he felt somewhat betrayed, but not because of the decision. He understood our business rationale although he may not have been in total agreement with it. He felt that way because I knew about the decision and I failed to tell him.

Deep down inside I think he felt as though I was abdicating my responsibility not only as a colleague, but more importantly as a friend, and in retrospect he was absolutely correct. In all the years that I have been in leadership positions, this is the one decision that I wish I could take back more than any other bad decision that I have made over the years. And let me assure you, I have made my fair share of bad decisions. The good news is that Sal has been gracious enough to put this one behind us. In other words, unlike his approach to his opponents on the golf course, Sal has given his friend a much-needed mulligan on this one.

It's interesting and very taxing to build personal relationships in the business world, especially when you lead those same people with whom you dine, party, play golf, or just hang out, but I would have it no other way. If I could repeat my career, I would not change it one bit in this regard. That is because I have found that those business associates who are closest to me personally—people like Kim, Ann Lloyd, Chris Carney, Scott Carmer, Dick Domann, John Delgiorno, Dan Long, Bill Leonard, and Sal—are the same ones who care enough to tell me the truth even in the most difficult situations. They have enriched my life.

Measuring this situation against the leadership values of integrity, courage, and empathy, it is easy to see how I could become seduced by the beauty of this ICE storm. It also, however, becomes very obvious how quickly I compromised those principles, and it becomes embarrassingly apparent how I risked the respect of one of my closest friends and co-workers that I had worked so hard to earn over the course of twenty years. Once the ice melts, the beauty disappears and the extent of the damage becomes very clear.

Let me take a minute or two to dissect the situation or, as those wonderful nuns at St. Philomena's would have said, "make a good examination of conscience." In other words, let me apply the individual components of the ICE model and benchmark my decisions and behaviors.

First from a perspective of integrity, I should have informed Sal myself about our decision and its ramifications on his situation. There should not have been a single moment of hesitation on my part. After all, we had been friends and associates for almost twenty years, and during that time we had leaned on each other often for support and counsel. My decision to put my head in the sand was clearly a violation of what I said in the chapter 4, "Par for the Course." In that chapter I refer to leaders who struggle with sharing bad news. I describe them as procrastinators who simply can't handle the task of facing individuals and telling them what they absolutely need to know. They are the ones who put it off or sweep it under the carpet with the hope that it will go away. They just do not understand that bad news is not like red wine; it does not get better with age. It almost always gets bitter with age.

Second, from the point of view of courage, I should have accepted responsibility for the decision. Leaders can and should take the heat. In this case I was running out of the kitchen. I went quiet when I should have spoken up. I allowed someone else to deliver a message that I should have delivered, and if you gave me truth serum, it was because I was afraid to deliver it. Deep down inside I knew there was a trade-off, and I made a decision to go "Teflon" on this one and take the easy way out.

In John F. Kennedy's Pulitzer Prize–winning book, *Profiles in Courage* (1956), Kennedy describes eight stories of senators who acted on principle and in the interest of our nation instead of acting in their own political interest. Each of the men Kennedy cites, people like Daniel Webster, sacrificed their own agenda to do what they believed was the right thing.

Finally, from a position of empathy or as my dad would say, "putting yourself in the shoes of the people you lead," my decision to go silent was one of insensitivity. Instead of leveraging the years of trust and respect between Sal and me and providing support to someone who was going to experience both professional and personal disruption, I was too focused on my own feelings of fear and how I was going to avoid this uncomfortable discussion. There is no doubt that mentors like Jim Butler or my father would have handled this completely differently. There is no doubt that my first boss, John Sweeney, would have invoked the face-in-the-mirror test not only as a test of integrity, but also as one of empathy. Each of them would have realized how important it is to stand tall and truly care about the feelings and situations of the people one leads.

No place on the globe is safe from natural disasters like tornadoes, hurricanes, volcanoes, and ice storms. And human beings, those social animals, live in groups just about everywhere on the face of the earth. Human beings are creatures of desires, not all of them altruistic; some desires are quite selfish. Therefore, just as we raid the supermarkets and horde supplies of food and flashlights in our homes to protect ourselves against the recurring power outages caused by ice storms here in North Carolina, we must also prepare, study, and relearn the ICE model in detail: what it can mean to us in an emotional emergency and how important it is to be prepared, not just in the dead of winter but all year long, for sudden (human) natural disasters like ICE storms.

You are loved for the little girl you were;
the special woman you are now, and the
precious daughter you will always be.

UNKNOWN

Chapter Twelve

———

DADDY'S LITTLE GIRL

$\mathcal{H}$aving spent countless hours writing this little book, I have struggled with how to end it. In the first place, I am not sure I really wanted to finish it. This piece of work has been my security blanket for the better part of three years or my personal Sigmund Freud. On many long jogs in cities throughout the world, it was my running companion as I thought of context and content by which I hoped to capture the reader's attention and make a positive impact on someone's approach to leadership. Before I knew it, four or five miles had flown by! Physically I felt exhilarated, knowing that I had burned some calories, and mentally I felt excited that I had structured some message or story during the jog.

Also, many evenings when I have returned home from the office or from another long business trip exhausted and frustrated from the challenges of our business, I've cracked open an ice-cold beer and put aside my cares and concerns by writing two or three pages. In many respects, working on this book has been the pharmaceutical I have needed. Medicine by metaphor, physician and novelist Walker Percy might have said. In 1976 he told an interviewer that stories, word-pictures, or metaphors "are very strange because when you put two things together, it's a way of discovering meanings [that] haven't been discovered before. It's a very strange thing because you discover meanings which you know, and the reader knows, but neither one of you knew that you knew until you see it discovered by a new metaphor," a new way of picturing an idea (*Conversations with Walker Percy*, 1985). So it was really healing and fun for me to put my stories and word-pictures together on the page—for you.

Additionally, I really struggled with how I should end it because I couldn't figure out what was *best* to convey in the last chapter. Day after day I churned through different metaphors, images, and stories that would *show* the best idea to leave you with at the close of this book. The first eleven chapters were easy. I have spoken both inside and outside my company so many times about things like passion, ICE, peer ceiling, and value creation that it was simply a matter of time and discipline to take those messages and stories and put them on paper.

The final chapter, however, is different. I wanted it to be a special finishing touch that would leave you totally convinced of how emotionally important practicing these values is to me, and how emotionally important practicing these values can be for you! So I searched the corners of my brain and the crevices of my memory for another message and story that would accomplish that goal. Was there something from my early childhood, my college days, my years at GlaxoSmithKline that would do the trick?

Was there another person I had not already described who had a serious impact on my life? Perhaps a teacher or a colleague or another friend? Nothing was clicking and I was getting frustrated. I wondered, *Did I really do justice in this book to the mentors in my life who helped me crystallize these values into practical leadership applications, or did I shortchange someone among them?*

I wanted to close out this book not only by feeling good about the messages and stories I had articulated in it, but also by knowing that those messages and stories had a real impact on the people I have had the privilege to lead. This final chapter needed to be an exclamation point on my many years in different leadership positions and on the valued lessons I learned from those whom I followed.

I felt confident that my work on this book was good. I asked friends to read it and constructively criticize it as it was being written. Their feedback was generally very positive. Sometimes on cross-continental flights, I would pull out a portion of the manuscript and start working on it. Invariably, the person next to me would get curious and ask, "What are you writing?" Always respectful, always polite, but deeply curious—people love stories.

I would answer them, and then I would use their question as a chance to solicit their opinions. Once again the feedback was good, and this was from complete strangers! So I knew that I had something. Everyone thought I had a good recipe of leadership themes and true stories constructed in an easy-to-read, straightforward, and memorable style. But it was missing that final message.

And to me eleven was an anticlimactic number of chapters to end on. I continued to search for the perfect metaphor, the most cogent ending, and I continued to come up empty.

Then it happened. I found it in the most obvious of places. It came to me on Father's Day directly from the heart of the most important mentor in my life, my daughter, Jackie. And it came to me in the form of a simple Father's Day card. Let me describe it.

On the cover of the card is a picture of a pretty little girl about seven years old. She is dressed in a knee-length white dress and she is dancing with her nattily dressed father. It reads:

> When
> I was little
> I looked up to you
> So much, Dad.
> I thought
> You were
> The strongest,
> Smartest,
> Most wonderful
> Dad
> In the world….

Inside the card, it continued:

> Now that I'm grown up
> I still feel that way.

That was enough to put me over the top. Even though those words pulled on my heartstrings and my eyes welled with tears, it wasn't until I looked farther down the card, however, and saw a handwritten note from Jackie that I got the best gift a daughter could give her dad.

As soon as I read it, I knew it was the perfect exclamation point for my book.

This is what she wrote:

> Daddy,
> This card seemed to jump out at me and it really is true. Each day I live my life in hopes to one day make and leave an impression on people the way you do. I know sometimes we may not see completely eye to eye, but I really do appreciate all the love and care that you have given me. I fortunately never have to question the love my parents have for me and I feel so blessed and thankful for that. Even though we did not get to spend Father's Day together, I really spend each day trying to live my life the same as the life you lead. You are my role model and an amazing person to look up to. Your Dad would be proud.
> I love you,
> Jackie

I carry that card with me everywhere I go. My friends, live like a leader. And pass it on. Put some ICE in your glass, feel free and refreshed, then drink deeply of clear, clear water.

About the Author

Steve Stefano, a graduate of St. Joseph's College, has been a senior executive at Glaxo since 1993. He is known mostly for his work in directing the company's commercial strategy and specifically its strategy with managed care customers.

Stefano is generally regarded as an expert in his field. He is a frequent speaker in the pharmaceutical industry and a regular lecturer on managed care strategy at such programs as the Wharton/Windhover Program and the Duke University Fuqua School of Business. He is known throughout his company and his industry as a colorful, pragmatic, and passionate leader of people.

Steve lives with his wife, Denise, in Cary, North Carolina. They have one daughter, Jackie, who was a four-year cheerleader at North Carolina State University and who now coaches cheerleading for the Wolfpack.